Criterion-Referenced Instruction

Criterion-Referenced Instruction

W. James Popham
Professor of Education
University of California, Los Angeles

FEARON PUBLISHERS

Lear Siegler, Inc., Education Division • Belmont, California

Preface

At a time when both prospective and practicing teachers are being subjected to ever-increasing scrutiny regarding the quality of their efforts, it is apparent that assistance must be provided for those engaged in designing and implementing instructional sequences. This book is designed for practicing teachers who wish to make more defensible decisions regarding their chief professional responsibilities, and for students of education who will soon be sharing those responsibilities. It is possible to place these professional decisions in three major categories—those which apply to *curriculum*, to *instruction*, and to *evaluation*. The organization of this book emphasizes these three primary areas of the educational process.

The purpose of the book is to help teachers develop tangible competencies that they can employ in discharging their curricular, instructional, and evaluational responsibilities. For this reason, specific instructional objectives describing these skills are presented in Part 1. Sample test items and practice exercises for each objective are provided to help the reader acquire the competencies that this book is attempting to promote. Part 3 supplies the information that the reader needs in order to acquire the intended competencies.

Because the book is organized around three major areas of education, and because it provides specific objectives associated with each of these areas, it is possible for the reader to focus his attention on only one area, if he wishes, or on two, or on all three. For instance, the teacher who is interested in improving his or her skill only in regard to curriculum decision making need complete only the sections of the book that are relevant to that topic.

This concise volume can be used to good advantage in teachers' workshops, institutes, and other in-service group activities. The unique organization of the book also makes it possible to use it without being formally involved with a pre-service or an in-service program. The book will be of particular value as a supplementary text in an instructional methodology course.

The assumption underlying this book is that improving the quality of the teacher's ability to make decisions in respect to curricular, instructional, and evaluational questions will bring about more appropriate teaching, which, in turn, will enable educators to achieve more defensible learner results.

With the taxpaying public more than ever committed to getting its money's worth from the public schools, members of the teaching profession are being required to develop *demonstratable* instructional skills. This book was written with the hope of helping teachers acquire these needed additional skills, which will lead to educational dividends for all learners.

W. James Popham

Contents

Part 1

Instructional Objectives

The following objectives represent many, but not all, of the goals that might be pursued in an instructional methodology course. The instructor for such a course can designate for his students those goals he wishes to pursue (or not pursue) in his course by having the students check the appropriate objects. Sample test items for these objectives are presented in Part 4 (page 49). The reader may wish to consult those items for further clarification of the objectives.

CURRICULUM

____ C- 1. *Measurable Objectives.* The student can correctly select from sets of educational objectives those which are stated in terms of measurable student behavior.

____ C- 2. *Writing Objectives.* The student can convert non-behavioral objectives to objective statements that adequately describe post-instruction behavior.

____ C- 3. *Content Generality.* The student can distinguish those objectives which possess content generality from those which possess test item equivalence.

____ C- 4. *Performance Standards.* The student can select from sets of educational objectives those which specify a minimally acceptable level (class and/or student minimal level[s]) of measurable performance.

___ C- 5. *Objective Domains.* Given a set of behavioral objectives, the student can classify each (a) according to whether it is primarily in the affective, psychomotor, or cognitive domain, and (b) if it is cognitive, according to whether it is the lowest level of that taxonomy or at a higher level.

___ C- 6. *Taxonomic Level.* Presented with a series of objectives and/ or test items, the student can identify which of four specific taxonomic levels (in multiple-choice alternatives) is represented.

___ C- 7. *Generating Objectives.* When presented with a previously unencountered non-behavioral objective in the affective or cognitive domain, the student can generate a number of measurable objectives reflecting that non-behavioral goal.

___ C- 8. *Ends and Means.* The student can distinguish between educational questions according to whether they are primarily related to ends or to means.

___ C- 9. *Tyler Rationale.* The learner can correctly match descriptive phrases with components of Ralph Tyler's curricular model (see pages 18–21).

___ C-10. *Preassessment.* Given descriptions of two or more teachers who are preassessing their pupils, the student can select the teacher making the appropriate inference and, subsequently, the correct instructional decision.

___ C-11. *Curriculum Terminology.* Given any of the curriculum terms in the Glossary (page 95), the student can correctly match each term with a paraphrased definition of the term.

INSTRUCTION

___ I- 1. *Instructional Principles.* Given two or more instructional principles, namely, (a) Revelation of Objectives, (b) Perceived Purpose, (c) Appropriate Practice, (d) Knowledge of Results, and a detailed description of a teacher's action in an instructional setting, the student can identify which of the principles, if any, the teacher is using.

___ I- 2. *Effective Instructional Principles.* Given a particular learning principle along with descriptions of two or more teachers' actions in an instructional setting, the student can select the teacher most effectively (presumptive effectiveness) incorporating the learning principle according to specified criteria.

_____ I- 3. *Teaching Assignments.* Given assignments to teach (a) classmates and/or (b) public school pupils, the student can plan and carry out learning activities which, insofar as the situation permits, incorporates the previously mentioned learning principles.

_____ I- 4. *Instructional Techniques.* Given descriptions of two or more teachers' use of one of four instructional techniques (lecture, discussion, demonstration, questioning), the student can select the teacher who is not violating one of the rules for that particular technique.

_____ I- 5. *Teaching Units.* The student can list and describe the recommended elements that should be included in teaching units.

_____ I- 6. *Lesson Plans.* The student can list and describe the recommended elements that should be included in lesson plans.

_____ I- 7. *Instructional Plans.* The student can distinguish among certain operations that should be carried out in developing (a) lesson plans, (b) teaching units, (c) both, or (d) neither.

_____ I- 8. *Discipline.* Given a description of a public school classroom in which poor discipline exists, the student can describe in writing at least four general principles and ten specific teacher actions that might result in improved discipline.

_____ I- 9. *Instructional Terminology.* Given any of the instruction terms in the Glossary, the student can correctly match each term with a paraphrased definition of the term.

EVALUATION

_____ E- 1. *Evaluative Decisions.* Given fictitious descriptions of pupil performance in an evaluation situation, the student can correctly select accurate inferences from several alternative interpretations.

_____ E- 2. *Testing Procedures.* Presented with descriptions of test construction, administration, scoring, and interpretation practices, the student can identify those generally approved by evaluation and measurement specialists.

—— E- 3. *Criterion Measures.* When presented with examples of diverse criterion measures, the student can classify each according to the following four categories: (a) learner behavior—natural conditions, (b) learner behavior—manipulated conditions, (c) learner product—natural conditions, and (d) learner product—manipulated conditions.

—— E- 4. *Writing Test Items.* The student can write test items that are congruent with a properly stated instructional objective.

—— E- 5. *Criterion- and Norm-Referenced Measurement.* The student can determine whether selected measurement operations are most appropriate for criterion-referenced or for norm-referenced testing.

—— E- 6. *Item Sampling.* The student can describe the basic procedure and reasons for constituting tests by item sampling.

—— E- 7. *Grading.* The student can distinguish between grading practices that are consistent with a criterion-referenced approach to instruction and those that are not.

—— E- 8. *Evaluation Terminology.* Given any of the evaluation terms in the Glossary, the student can correctly match each term with a paraphrased definition of the term.

Part 2

Content Outline

Each of the topics in the following outline is treated in the expository section of the text which follows. In a typical instructional methodology class, of course, most of the topics will be treated in more detail. The course instructor may wish to designate which topics will be emphasized (or de-emphasized) by having his students check certain of the topics in the spaces provided.

I. INTRODUCTION

___ A. Teaching viewed as an activity amenable to systematic improvement

___ B. An empirically based instructional paradigm

    ___ 1. Curriculum considerations: ends

    ___ 2. Instruction considerations: means

    ___ 3. Evaluation considerations: recycling

II. CURRICULUM

___ A. Generation or selection of objectives as the initial task

___ B. Specification of objectives in measurable terms

    ___ 1. Test item equivalence

    ___ 2. Content generality

___ C. Establishing performance standards for objectives

     ___ 1. Student minimum levels

     ___ 2. Class minimum levels

___ D. Ralph Tyler's curriculum rationale

___ E. The Taxonomies of Educational Objectives

     ___ 1. Cognitive

     ___ 2. Affective

     ___ 3. Psychomotor

___ F. Necessity of preassessment

     ___ 1. Techniques of pre-testing

     ___ 2. Uses of pre-test data

III. INSTRUCTION

___ A. Adherance to learning principles

     ___ 1. Revelation of objectives

     ___ 2. Perceived purpose

     ___ 3. Appropriate practice

     ___ 4. Knowledge of results

___ B. Task analysis

___ C. Written plans

     ___ 1. Teaching units

     ___ 2. Lesson plans

___ D. Rules of thumb for teacher-directed instructional techniques

     ___ 1. Lecture

     ___ 2. Demonstration

     ___ 3. Discussion

     ___ 4. Questioning

___ E. Discipline

     ___ 1. General principles

     ___ 2. Specific techniques

IV. EVALUATION

___ A. Differing conceptions of evaluation

     ___ 1. Outcome-oriented models

     ___ 2. Information–decision-making models

_____ B. Formative and summative evaluation
_____ C. Measurement considerations
          _____ 1. Norm-referenced measurement
          _____ 2. Criterion-referenced measurement
          _____ 3. Classes of criterion measures
          _____ 4. Test construction
          _____ 5. Item sampling
_____ D. Grading
_____ E. Assessing teaching proficiency

Part 3

Criterion-Referenced Instruction

There are a number of ways of thinking about instruction. Some of them are conducive to instructional improvement. Others are not. For example, some people view teaching as a largely artistic endeavor that defies any attempt at systematic analysis. From this point of view the good teacher is quite literally born, not made, and one can do little to improve a teacher's proficiency other than yearn for retroactive genetic modifications. An alternative view of teaching holds that there are identifiable portions of the instructional act that are amenable to rigorous analysis and subsequent improvement. It is the latter view of instruction on which this book is based.

Any person who sets out systematically to improve his teaching skill is embarking on a challenging but rewarding task. And this does not suggest that the only people who set out to think rigorously about instruction are *prospective* teachers. Many *experienced* teachers come to realize that their approaches to instruction have been largely instinctual. Even seasoned veteran teachers can profit by approaching the instructional act with a degree of precision.

There are a variety of dimensions in which the truly excellent teacher undoubtedly excells, such as personality, intelligence, speaking proficiency, and so on. Some of these variables, however, are less amenable to change than others. There is one area in which the teacher can improve himself quite dramatically—namely, that of *instructional decision making*. An instructor must make innumerable decisions before, during, and after a given instructional sequence. Certain decisions must be made regarding what should be taught, how it should be taught, and how the teaching procedures should be evaluated after they have been concluded. These are intellectual decisions made by an instructor (or an instructional team). To the degree that those decisions are made wisely, the quality of the teacher's instruction and the learners' achievements will be augmented.

A Criterion-Referenced Instructional Paradigm

The approach to instruction endorsed in this book is based on the central premise that the reason for a teacher's being in the classroom is to bring about a change in the learners. A teacher may be able to lecture with the eloquence of Cicero and lead discussions with the consummate skill of Carl Rogers. But if his students leave the classroom essentially unchanged, then, in spite of his apparent attributes, the teacher is a failure. We are in the business of education to improve our learners, and improvement requires change. Thus, an appropriate view of instruction demands that we emphasize the nature of the changes that occur in learners. Since behavioral modifications can be considered the standard or *criterion* by which we judge instruction, it is possible to focus during the entire instructional act on such a criterion. More simply, such an approach can be referred to as a *criterion-referenced instructional scheme*.

The instructional model or paradigm advocated here is a relatively simple criterion-referenced scheme because, quite frankly, the more complex an instructional model is, the less likely it is to be widely used. Although it is true that it is possible to analyze instructional operations with hyper-sophistication, classifying myriad instructional variables according to their intermittent occurrence per millisecond, few teachers have the time for such complex approaches. It is far better to present a less esoteric scheme that can be realistically used by busy teachers. The scheme proposed in this book has been employed with success by a variety of instructors, and can be used profitably by any teacher who wishes to adopt a systematic approach to improving his classroom performance. The major components of this instructional paradigm include objectives, preassessment, instruction, and evaluation (see Figure 1). Although each of these four components will be treated in more detail later, a brief examination is in order now.

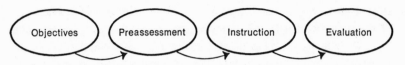

FIGURE 1   Major Components of a Criterion-Referenced
Instructional Paradigm

Curriculum Considerations. Because the focus of this instructional model is on the criterion—that is, the behavior of the learner—it is crucial to identify the intended behavioral changes at the outset of instruction. Thus, the first element of this instructional model is the specification of instructional objectives.

Once these objectives have been described as clearly as possible, the learner is then measured (preassessed) to find out where he stands in relation to these objectives. It is important to determine before the instruction begins that the learner cannot already perform the behaviors we intend to promote. It is equally important to find out if he has the prerequisite ability or learning that will enable him to achieve those particular objectives. On the basis of the preassessment, the objectives may be modified in order to make them more consistent with the learner's entry behavior.

These two components, objectives and preassessment, constitute the curriculum phase of this instructional paradigm. As such, they are concerned with the *ends* of education. They are concerned with what ought to be the goals of the instructional sequence. In large measure, these two components are not attentive to the question of instructional *means*— that is, how to accomplish specified ends.

Instructional Considerations. The third component of the instructional paradigm consists of designing an instructional sequence that will enable the learner to achieve the instructional objectives. Instruction represents the procedure or means by which we hope to promote our educational intentions. There are a number of instructional principles that can be used in the selection of learning activities and, as we shall see, there are techniques for subsequently verifying the adequacy of these decisions.

Evaluation Considerations. At the conclusion of the instructional sequence, the fourth component of the instructional paradigm is considered, namely, evaluation. Evaluation in this sense is not an evaluation of the learners—that is, it is not concerned with whether we give grades of A or B to particular students. Rather, it is an attempt to assess the quality of instructional decision making that has occurred up to that time. The purpose of evaluation in this case is to give the teacher an opportunity to carefully reconsider his instructional performance on the basis of empirical evidence so that, if necessary, modifications can be made in his curricular and instructional decisions. The evaluation is made primarily in terms of the learner's post-instruction attainment of the intended objectives, and it is for this reason that the entire instructional model is considered a criterion-referenced scheme.

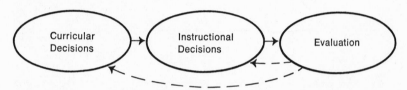

FIGURE 2   Self-Correcting Elements of a Criterion-Referenced
Instructional Model

On the basis of an evaluation made of the learner's post-instruction behavior, the teacher is able to reconsider the quality of his curricular decisions as well as his instructional decisions and to correct deficiencies in those decisions. It is for this reason, of course, that the model is referred to as a self-correcting system (see Figure 2). The use of such a system requires a teacher who has a fair amount of ego strength. Decisions, once reached, are not automatically bronzed for posterity. There is a healthy atmosphere of doubt regarding the quality of one's instructional and curricular decisions. Only when empirical evidence shows that decisions are sound does the teacher reach some degree of certainty regarding those decisions.

We see, then, that there are three major kinds of professional activities in which a teacher is engaged: those related to *curriculum, instruction,* and *evaluation.* The remainder of this text is organized under these three general rubrics, and the various instructional objectives that this book attempts to promote are classified under these three headings, as are the sample test items, practice exercises, and bibliographic entries.

CURRICULUM

The Initial Task: Determining the Instructional Objectives

The first step in a criterion-referenced instructional model is to decide on the objectives that the instruction is designed to promote. Most educators agree that educational objectives are important. They will readily agree that the teacher does not really know what to do without instructional goals, that he does not really know what to plan for in his classes without them. Unfortunately, however, most instructional objectives are stated so vaguely and so ambiguously that they are of limited value. When objectives are phrased in very broad terms, there are many possible interpretations that could be made about what they mean and it becomes almost impossible to figure out what the instructor really has in mind. For example, when a teacher says he wants his students to "become familiar with" a certain concept, we do not know how they are supposed to manifest this familiarity unless the instructor goes on to state just what the students should be able to do in order to evidence the desired familiarity.

Measurable Objectives. Meaningful instructional objectives must be stated in terms of student behavior, and they must specify the type of behavior a student will engage in (or be able to engage in) when he has satisfactorily achieved the objective. For instance, the teacher might assert first in a rather general way that the student will "understand" a particular principle, and then he might clarify this goal by giving a more specific objective. This objective could indicate, for example, that understanding will be manifested when the student is able to describe in writing the five major elements of the principle and give one original example of each.

In other words, the more explicit the instructor can be regarding the statement of instructional objectives, the better. The only kind of specificity that really helps in improving teacher behavior empirically is the specification of goals in terms of student behavior changes. "Behavior" in this sense is defined rather broadly. It does not need to be behavior only on a test; it may also include behavior in an informal situation (for example, observed politeness) or even behavior in a situation specifically contrived by the instructor to reflect a *more basic kind* of commitment. For instance, the literature instructor is often concerned with the degree to which his students are really interested in the literature he has been treating. He may set up situations in which students are free to choose reading material, and he may then note the degree to which their choices coincide with preferences advocated in his class. The behavior used most commonly to measure behaviorally stated objectives is test behavior, although there are numerous other ways to assess objectives in the intellectual as well as attitudinal realms. These latter approaches take considerable ingenuity on the part of the teacher. Some suggestions regarding non-standard approaches to test construction are offered in the evaluation section (page 40).

By practicing the writing of objectives in measurable terms, the teacher can become skilled at describing his intentions in such a way that it is possible to measure them. And whether the objectives are referred to as "behavioral objectives," "operational objectives," or "performance objectives," they all have one feature in common: they are *measurable*. But even though the teacher can become skilled at this task, it is an extremely time-consuming operation. There are other courses of action available in deciding upon instructional goals. For instance, such agencies as the Instructional Objectives Exchange[1] maintain large "banks" of instructional objectives from which the teacher may *select* objectives that are appropriate to his own instructional situation. By selecting objectives rather than generating them himself, the teacher is relieved of the responsibility of preparing exhaustive (and exhausting) sets of instructional objectives, but he can still direct his instructional efforts toward measurable goals. Only a fraction of the available goals need be selected, and the teacher is always free to supplement them with his own. Such agencies as the Instructional Objectives Exchange offer teachers a valuable service with respect to the identification of instructional intentions.

Content Generality

Early proponents of measurable objectives were often so concerned with the necessity for precision in stating an objective that they advocated objectives that were essentially nothing more than test items. Objectives like "The student will be able to list the names of five U.S. presidents" were

---

[1]Information regarding the objectives available from the Instructional Objectives Exchange may be secured from that agency: Instructional Objectives Exchange, Box 24095, Los Angeles, Calif. 90024.

considered acceptable and, with respect only to measurability, they were indeed acceptable. Unfortunately, since these objectives were really *test item equivalents,* most teachers would be obliged to have literally hundreds of such objectives for a given course. It was clear that to be of more utility an instructional objective had to cover a *class* of learner behaviors rather than a *single* test item. Thus, teachers are now urged to use instructional objectives that possess *content generality*—that is, objectives that describe behaviors that can generalize across a range of content. For instance, consider the following objective: "The learner will be able to add correctly any pair of four-digit numbers." Or, examine this one: "The student will be able to spell aloud correctly any twenty words randomly drawn from a list of five hundred 'hard' spelling words." Both of these objectives possess content generality and, while measurable, possess the advantage of covering a range of learner behaviors rather than a single test item response.

Some instructional objectives might, of course, be measurable only by a single item. For example, a track coach might want his hundred-yard-dash men to run one hundred yards in less than ten seconds on at least one occasion in their lives. In such instances, of course, a test item equivalent objective is acceptable. However, the teacher will ordinarily find more utility in content general objectives.

Performance Standards

It is also extremely important to specify minimally acceptable standards for the performance of the student. These standards should be described *in advance* of the instruction. With clear criterion levels, the teacher can attempt to gear his instruction so that the students will be able to behave as well as initially specified before the instruction begins. In other words, he should certify in advance *how well* students must do on the behavioral measures in order for his instruction to be considered satisfactory. It is extremely difficult, particularly for the beginning teacher, to establish precisely how well students should do on examinations or other behavioral measures. However, in time, it is usually possible to reach a more or less defensible decision regarding the minimum proficiency students should display on assessment devices. The teacher can then pit his instructional effectiveness against these standards.

In some cases, the minimum standards are rather well established by the fact that the student goes on to an advanced class that requires certain prerequisite knowledge and skills. In other, professional types of courses, the necessary proficiency of the student can be validated against the actual performance requirements of the job. For example, medical schools have an enormously important criterion for their programs—the life, or death, of patients depends on their doctors' proficiency. Therefore, in certain surgery courses, it is necessary to establish 100 percent accuracy on particular kinds of skill tests, whereas in other fields less than perfect accuracy may be acceptable.

Student Minimal Levels. The first kind of performance standard that must be explicated concerns how well an individual learner should be able to perform a particular behavior. For example, suppose that we are trying to determine how well a student must be able to spell. Given twenty words randomly selected from a list of five hundred, how many must the child spell correctly in order for his performance to be considered acceptable? We might assert that a 50 percent proficiency level is demanded and that he, therefore, must spell at least ten of twenty words correctly to be considered acceptable. Or we might set an 80 percent proficiency level or even a 100 percent level. In any event, we must indicate exactly how well an individual student must perform in order for his response to be considered acceptable. This performance standard is referred to as a *student minimal level.*

Class Minimal Levels. In addition to a student minimal level, the teacher is anxious to determine how well a *group* of students must perform in order for his instruction to be considered successful. It is, therefore, necessary to establish a *class minimal level* which indicates what percentage of the class must perform at a specified student minimal level of proficiency. For example, the teacher might describe his objectives in the following terms: "At least 70 percent of the class will answer 80 percent or more of the multiplication problems correctly." Notice that this objective establishes both a student and a class minimal level of proficiency. Indeed, for a properly stated class minimal standard, there *must* be a student minimal standard. For instance, it would not make much sense to say that 90 percent of the class ought to be able to "do well" on the exercises. Unless a student minimal level has been established, a class minimal level does not help a teacher. It is also important to note that unless the objective is stated in measurable terms, neither the class nor the student minimal level is meaningful.

Another characteristic of a well-stated objective is that it specifies any important condition under which the criterion behavior will be displayed. In other words, any "givens" or restrictions that will actually make a difference in expected learner performance after instruction should be identified. To illustrate, if the student is to take an open-book test, then the availability of the book should be described. If, in a mathematics class, the student is required to use certain mathematical formulas rather than others, this condition should also be described. However, in comparison with the importance of specifying measurable behavior and performance standards, the descriptions of condition are of far less importance. If a teacher can explicate his objectives in measurable terms and can indicate the level of proficiency he expects the learner to display, he undoubtedly possesses useful objectives. If there are significant conditions that should be described within the objectives, it would, of course, be desirable to state them.

Promoting Which Objectives?

Once it has been decided that specific, measurable objectives have some instructional utility, it must next be decided what kinds of objectives should be sought. What goals or aims should be endorsed by the schools? One of the greatest dangers of behaviorizing our desired instructional outcomes is that those goals most amenable to measurement are usually the most trivial. How can we avoid unimportant goals and select objectives that are really worthwhile? The danger of any effective instructional approach is that we may be teaching the wrong things. One of the consoling features of ineffectual instruction is that a weak teacher does not have to care too much about which goals he selects because his students aren't going to learn much anyway. Criterion-referenced instruction is too powerful to use with inadequate objectives.

As indicated earlier, although there is some overlap, it is helpful to think of instructional objectives as the task of the curriculum maker and the selection of procedures for achieving those objectives as the task of the instructional specialist. In other words, when we are considering *what* we should teach (ends), we are primarily engaged in the field of curriculum; when we are deciding *how* we should teach (means), we are concerned more with instruction.

The Tyler Rationale

There are at least two ways of looking at instructional objectives so that we avoid unimportant goals. The first of these is by the use of a curricular approach such as the one advocated by Ralph Tyler.[2] According to this scheme, a teacher decides on instructional objectives by first consulting three sources: the student, the society, and the subject matter. Having selected possible objectives from these three sources, he then scrutinizes his objectives in terms of two screens, the psychology of learning and a philosophy of education. The objectives that pass these screens are then behaviorized and used to guide the nature of the instruction.

The first source of tentative objectives is the student himself. By analyzing his needs, we may reach certain generalizations suggesting possible objectives for instruction. By analyzing the needs of the learner and discovering the difference between his present condition and an acceptable norm, we may decide whether to pay attention to the student's health, for example, or to his moral deficiencies. Perhaps the interests of the learner suggest that we use certain intriguing topics as points of departure for our instruction. In general, we are forced to compare the learner's needs and interests with some kinds of norms to interpret whether our generalizations are acceptable. In other words, collecting information about students does not automatically yield objectives; rather, it only makes possible certain suggestions for objectives.

One way to practice using this particular source is to consider students at a grade level we are familiar with and to outline the kinds of investigations that would have to be conducted in order to learn more about their needs and interests. By considering even hypothetical data of this kind, the teacher should be able to practice generating potential objectives drawn from an analysis of the learners themselves. It is sometimes possible for

---

[2]Ralph W. Tyler, *Basic Principles of Curriculum and Instruction* (Chicago: University of Chicago Press, 1950).

the teacher to recall his own needs and interests during his public school years, and these recollections may also suggest possible objectives drawn from the learner as a source.

A second possible source of objectives is the society. There are several arguments for studying our society and deciding on objectives in terms of what the society requires of the schools. However, because of the ever-changing nature of the culture, transitory aspects of society that will soon be out of date should not be emphasized. Even so, there are criticisms of "presentism" based on an analysis of the *status quo,* but it has been suggested that these criticisms are not valid if society's status is only one of the sources of our objectives.

Often a societal analysis is conducted in terms of what people actually do. These activities can be classified by a number of schemes, and on the basis of these classifications curricular goals can be suggested. Once more, it is necessary to apply some sort of norm to the interpretation of data drawn from the society; the conditions of the society do not automatically determine our goals. However, by analyzing the society's needs, we will probably discover, among other things, that many people in the society believe that the school is set up and financed by the society as an agency to preserve and, possibly, to enhance our culture. This belief should suggest certain curricular objectives.

A third source of curricular objectives is the subject matter. This is perhaps the most common source, and subject specialists with extensive knowledge of their own fields may suggest certain objectives that are suitable in terms of the student's comprehension of the discipline. Subject matter specialists have frequently concerned themselves only with the development of other specialists in their own fields. In recent years, however, we have seen some refreshing changes, and the modern specialist often promotes the contribution of his field to the life of the ordinary citizen.[3] Good sources for objectives in the subject field are the national councils of teacher specialist groups—the national councils of mathematics teachers, English teachers, social studies teachers, and so on. These groups

---

[3]See John I. Goodlad, *School Curriculum Reform in the United States* (New York: The Fund for the Advancement of Education, 1964).

often make recommendations regarding what should be taught. Their objectives are generally derived from an analysis of the discipline in question.

Once we have examined our three sources, we are in a position to make a collection of tentative objectives—perhaps ten or so from each source. But it is quite clear that for any given course, over a year or a semester, it is impossible to accomplish as much as might be suggested by these three sources, for only a limited amount of pupil behavior can be changed in a relatively short period. Many teachers "cover all the material" without realizing that their coverage often results in very little behavior change on the part of their pupils. Thus the teacher should establish a hierarchy of importance with respect to his objectives and should attempt to implement only those which are important and have a reasonable chance of being achieved. At this point we should subject the objectives we have accumulated to the two screens suggested by the Tyler Rationale. Only those objectives which satisfactorily pass through the screens should be actually used by the teacher.

The first screen is the psychology of learning. The primary function of this screen is to eliminate those objectives which cannot be learned in the time available. We can discover through certain research studies in the field of learning that some objectives cannot be achieved in the school. For example, profound personality modifications, perhaps possible in early stages of the child's development, are nearly impossible to bring about in the high school or junior college. The more sophisticated the teacher's understanding of the psychology of learning, the more adeptly this screen can be employed. One of the purposes of educational psychology classes should be to enable the teacher to use the psychology of learning to screen out objectives with a low probability of achievement for his classes. Through the judicious use of the psychology of learning screen, one would expect a number of objectives previously suggested by the three sources to be excluded.

The second screen is the instructor's philosophy of education. Most teachers do not have a systematic philosophy of education, but rather possess a collection of more or less consistent beliefs regarding what the schools should do. A teacher's values will obviously influence the kinds of objectives he eventually selects, and by using the philosophical screen he will eliminate a number of the objectives that have been suggested. For

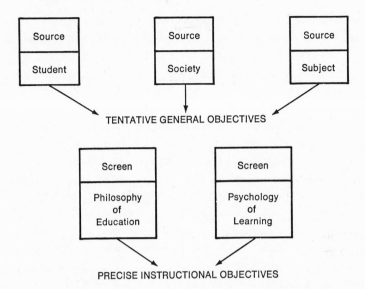

FIGURE 3   Schematic Representation of the Tyler Rationale

instance, in the extreme, it is conceivable that a philosophical screen might exclude all the objectives based on the learner himself if the teacher considers this an irrelevant source of objectives. More often than not, certain objectives remain from each source, but perhaps one or two sources are emphasized.

After these two screenings, a collection of residual objectives will remain, and these are the ones the teacher will try to implement. By using an approach such as this, the teacher will be more circumspect in his selection of objectives that if he merely sat down and tried to decide what to teach "from scratch." This is, perhaps, the greatest advantage of a systematic curricular rationale. Schematically, the Tyler Rationale can be depicted as seen in Figure 3.

It is possible to apply the two screens before even considering the three sources. Further, we need not use the screens or sources in the precise order described here. Regardless of the sequence, however, the consideration of these several elements in deriving measurable instructional objectives should at least partially counteract the tendency to select only the easily measured, hence possibly the least important, objectives.

Taxonomies of Educational Objectives

Another way to avoid trivial objectives and to select judiciously those objectives which should actually be taught is to analyze our objectives in terms of the Taxonomies of Educational Objectives. These taxonomies were developed by a group of people who isolated objectives into three major domains—the cognitive, the affective, and the psychomotor. Taxonomies (classifications) of educational objectives for the cognitive and affective domains have been widely used for the last several years.[4]

In essence, both taxonomies attempt to classify objectives according to hierarchies. In the case of the cognitive domain, for instance, a hierarchy of *intellectual* behavior is developed that ranges from (1) knowledge, to (2) comprehensive, to (3) application, to (4) analysis, to (5) synthesis, and, finally, to (6) evaluation. In the affective domain, which deals with attitudes, feelings, interests, the categorization scheme ranges from (1) receiving, to (2) responding, to (3) valuing, to (4) organizing, to (5) characterization. In both instances, one's objectives should probably not all be at the lowest levels of the sequence. In other words, if we classify our cognitive objectives and find that they are almost exclusively knowledge objectives, then we should have some doubts as to whether that is what we ought to be teaching.

The major value of the affective taxonomy is that it points out the fact that instructors characteristically overlook objectives having to do with attitudes, interests, emotions, and so on. Just being aware that this domain has been overlooked is often of benefit to the teacher by suggesting the addition of such objectives.

With respect to the cognitive domain, the major fact usually revealed by analyzing our objectives with this device is that the majority of the objectives are at the lowest level of that domain, namely, rote (memorized) knowledge. It is conceivable, therefore, to compress the cognitive taxonomy to only two levels, that is, (1) knowledge and (2) anything higher than knowledge. Even this gross, two-category system will reveal the pro-

---

[4]Benjamin S. Bloom *et al., Taxonomy of Educational Objectives: Handbook I, Cognitive Domain* (New York: David McKay Co., 1956); David R. Krathwohl, Benjamin S. Bloom, and Bertram B. Masia, *Taxonomy of Educational Objectives: Handbook II, Affective Domain* (New York: David McKay Co., 1964).

portion of a teacher's objectives at higher levels and should help him to avoid the pursuit of trivial goals.

One problem with the Taxonomies of Educational Objectives is that they were devised before educators began to look for instructional objectives that were completely measurable. Some of the classifications and examples in the cognitive and affective taxonomies, therefore, lack the degree of precision we might now desire. Further, there are some educators who resist these taxonomies on the grounds that it is impossible to classify learner behavior as exclusively cognitive rather than, for example, as cognitive *plus* affective *plus* psychomotor. Surely, there are admixtures of all of the three domains in almost all learner behaviors, but if the emphasis is on the type of domain primarily represented by a given behavior, these taxonomies can be of some use to the teacher.

Preassessment

In effective instruction it is first necessary to preassess the student to determine his status in regard to the instructional objectives. In other words, the teacher should attempt to identify the learner's entry behavior. The term "preassessment" is used rather than "pre-testing" only because preassessment may suggest a more generally applicable assessment procedure than the use of paper-and-pencil tests. One of the real advantages of preassessment is discovering whether the student's background includes the kind of behavior the teacher wishes to promote. It is conceivable that students may enter the course with far more competence than is assumed by the instructor, and weeks may be wasted in "teaching" students something they already know. In the same vein, it is often the case that students know far less than we assume they know. They may actually fail to possess the prerequisite abilities, knowledge, or skills they need to achieve the course objectives.

In either case, preassessment results may suggest modifications of the originally selected objectives, with respect to both the minimal levels and the actual content of the objectives themselves. For instance, an analysis of the student's entry behavior may suggest that the teacher should add or delete objectives. In other cases it might be prudent to alter only the minimal levels previously established for the objectives.

no external validity

$?$

A particularly important advantage of preassessing is that we can establish with certainty that the student cannot, in advance of instruction, perform well with respect to the objectives. When, after instruction, he is able to behave in the prescribed fashion, the teacher's instructional efforts will deserve credit for bringing about the behavior change. This point will be discussed in more detail later in the section on evaluation (page 40).

An additional advantage of preassessment is that we can use it to identify individual students for whom we may wish to differentiate our instruction. For remarkably able students, we might select objectives that are different from those for the rest of the class in order to give these special students different instructional experiences.

The actual preassessment may be conducted either formally, as with a paper-and-pencil test, or quite informally. When, for example, a new class in the Russian language is instituted in a high school, perhaps the only kind of preassessment necessary is for the teacher to ask which students know the Russian language. If no one knows it, the teacher can proceed with the assumption of no knowledge on the part of the students. Ideally, preassessment devices should take the same form as those used in final evaluation. Perhaps the pre-test, if it is a test, should be the same as the post-test. It is obvious that, in order to consider preassessment, the instructor must already have given serious attention to the question of final assessment. Once having preassessed his students, and possibly having modified his objectives accordingly, the instructor is now ready to begin planning the instructional activities which he hopes will enable his students to achieve the objectives.

INSTRUCTION

Once the objectives have been determined, the teacher's task is to design an instructional sequence that represents his best judgment regarding the means of achieving those objectives. In other words, the teacher is now faced with the job of deciding what will actually happen during the class period—and this means planning what will happen during particular minutes of the class period. Many beginning teachers make this decision on the most opportunistic grounds, hoping that whatever they do that *seems* educational will, in fact, result in learning. In the instructional paradigm advocated here, we offer four learning principles to guide the teacher in selecting his classroom activities. These learning principles have considerable support from the field of psychology, and it is probable that, by using them, the teacher will be able to provide more suitable learning experiences for youngsters than he otherwise could. There are certainly more than four principles that could be described. But by becoming thoroughly conversant with the four presented here, the teacher will be in a better position to augment his arsenal of instructional tactics thereafter.

Before discussing the four principles, we should distinguish between *use* and *effective use* of a principle. It is clear that some principles can be used, and clearly used at that, but used in a fashion that is not particularly effective. Drawing an analogy from the field of sports, we might think of a novice tennis player who is attempting to use a principle on the proper way to hit a backhand shot. We observe him on the court and see him hit the ball over the net. Now, did he use the principle on which the appropriate backhand stroke was based? Perhaps he did. However, if we ask ourselves whether he used it very effectively—whether he has an effective backhand shot—we might have to answer no, for he might only have used the principle on one occasion. Thus, a distinction can be drawn between use and effectiveness.

However, it is often impossible to determine in advance just what factors should be involved in certain instructional principles to make their use effective. The best we can do is to offer suggestions regarding factors that presumably affect the effectiveness of a particular principle. The ultimate test of whether a principle has been effectively used must be conducted in terms of the terminal behavioral change of the pupils. Some teachers who violate the suggestions about how a principle is used effectively may actually modify the behavior of their students in a desired direction. Similarly, some tennis players violate basic stroke principles, yet they are always able to return the ball across the net. Who is to say that they do not have an "effective" stroke? The distinction drawn here is between use and *presumptive* effectiveness. In the practice exercise (Part 5, page 57), the reader is asked to identify teachers who use certain instructional principles and, in addition, to identify teachers who use the principles effectively. Please recall that *effectiveness* refers to presumptive effectiveness, and that this effectivness must be tested ultimately in an empirical fashion.

Revelation of Objectives. Although it may sound theological, the first instructional principle possesses a number of real-world advantages. It merely involves informing the students of the goals of the instructional sequence. Once the teacher has clarified for himself the nature of his instructional intentions, having specified them in terms of measurable learner outcomes, why not let the students in on the secret? Many studies have dramatically demonstrated that a learner will accomplish instructional objectives more effectively when he is clear about the nature of those goals. This should be obvious, for students usually spend far too much time trying to guess how the instructor will test them.

One simple way of communicating instructional objectives to older students is to give them an actual copy of the course objectives at the beginning of the school year. If there are a great many objectives and the teacher thinks that the students would be overwhelmed by them, it might be better to hand out small numbers of objectives to cover limited periods of time. For example, the teacher might give the students only the objectives covering a single teaching unit at the beginning of that teaching unit.

It is particularly important to communicate objectives to learners in language that they understand. Therefore, a teacher would be presumed to be using this principle more effectively if he transmitted the objectives in language comprehensible to the students. To give very young children—for example, second graders—complicated statements of instructional objectives that might have been written originally for the teacher's professional colleagues would clearly be an ineffective use of this principle. With very young learners, it would perhaps be better to give examples of the kinds of skills they will acquire at the end of an instructional period—that is, to show them the kinds of words they will be able to read or indicate the kinds of arithmetic problems they will be able to solve.

Another presumptive-effectiveness criterion to be used with the revelation-of-objectives principle is related to revealing the objectives early. It would do little good, of course, to reveal objectives to learners only minutes before the final examination. The best use of this principle requires that it be used as early in an instructional sequence as possible.

Some teachers may wish to involve learners in the selection of instructional objectives. Other teachers will not wish to do so. Either position reflects a philosophic stance that can be well defended. Some teachers may even want to inform parents of the nature of their instructional goals. By having a precise collection of objectives and by getting the reactions of others to these goals, the teacher will be in a better position to make judgments regarding what might be reasonable instructional intentions for his class. The more reasonable the intentions, of course, the more power the revelation-of-objectives principle will have. This relates to a second instructional principle, namely, perceived purpose.

Perceived Purpose.   According to this principle, we try to promote the student's perception of the purpose or value of the learning activity. Many teachers assume, in error, that their students automatically understand why they are studying a particular topic. In fact, many students have great difficulty in discerning why they are being forced to attend to certain subject matters. In using this principle, the teacher attempts to establish a "set" or predisposition which increases the student's inclination to learn.

There is considerable research evidence suggesting that students who see a real purpose in learning something will learn it better. To illustrate, it is often said that some of the worst instruction takes place in medical schools, where instructors are frequently selected because of their medical proficiency rather than their instructional prowess. However, the prospective physician usually learns very well because he is so highly motivated to succeed in the school, having recognized the obvious rewards of the medical profession.

The principle of perceived purpose can be employed with only modest effort in some cases, but many experienced school supervisors indicate that it is the principle most frequently overlooked by beginning teachers. The teacher tends to think that his students understand why the topic they are studying is worthwhile. This is usually not so.

There are several methods of promoting the students' perception of the value of the subject matter. The teacher can do this by a rather straightforward explanation of why the subject matter will be important to them. This is referred to as promoting perceived purpose through *deduction*.

The teacher might also wish the students themselves to infer why the objectives are important. This is referred to as promoting perceived purpose through *induction*. The teacher can also hold out the promise of good grades or some other reward and thus promote perceived purpose through the use of *extrinsic rewards*. The teacher might also merely urge the students to "study diligently" or to "work hard," thereby promoting perceived purpose through *exhortation*. Whether through deduction, induction, extrinsic rewards, or exhortation (or possibly a combination of these), the teacher should attempt to increase the students' motivation to achieve the instructional objectives.

The first presumptive effectiveness criterion for this principle pertains to the time sequence in which it is used. If the perceived-purpose activity is going to be valuable, it should be employed near the beginning of a unit or lesson so that, even before the student starts to study, he understands why it is important for him to learn. Second, the degree to which the teacher attempts to communicate perceived purpose is an important criterion of effectiveness. A teacher who walks into an English class and tells the students to study grammar because it is "good for them" probably communicates very ineffectively to the class even though he is using the principle of perceived purpose. The teacher must discover ways to reach the student and suggest to him why the subject he is studying is of value. If the student understands how the subject material is relevant to his everyday experience, he will attempt to master it with far more enthusiasm than if vague abstractions are used for justification. Then, too, perceived purpose should occasionally be used after the instruction has begun in order to remind the student of the importance of the objectives.

Appropriate Practice. A particularly powerful instructional principle is that the student must have an opportunity to practice the kind of behavior implied by the objective. That is, he must be given practice appropriate to the objective. There is a host of psychological literature that suggests that if we wish the student to behave in a particular fashion, we must give him a chance to respond actively. If this response is consistent with our aims, all the better.

If an algebra teacher, for instance, wishes a student to manifest knowledge of the subject matter by solving story problems, then he should not give him only equations to practice throughout the course. Rather, he should give him practice in solving story problems.

A particularly interesting point arises in connection with the judgment of whether certain practice is "appropriate." In order to judge conclusively whether practice is appropriate, we must have a behavioral objective. Take, for instance, a non-behavioral objective such as "The student will understand algebra." If we were to walk into a school classroom and see an algebra class engaged in certain activities, we would not be certain whether those activities were appropriate to a desired objective because we would not know with certainty what the desired objective was. We would not know what criterion of understanding was to be employed. At best, we would not be sure if the practice was appropriate. Hence, for all practical purposes, we must find a behavioral objective in order to assert conclusively that appropriate practice is present.

The beginning teacher will usually find that this is the single most important principle in securing a desired behavior change. Many neophyte teachers wonder in amazement when students fail to perform well on tests; they have spent the entire time lecturing, sometimes even eloquently, but they have not given the students the opportunity to respond during class. Through the use of the principle of appropriate practice, real behavior changes can usually be accomplished.

Giving the learner an opportunity to practice behavior exactly like the class of behaviors called for in the instructional objective is referred to as *equivalent practice*. Giving the learner an opportunity to practice behavior that is comparable, but not exactly the same as that called for in the objective, is called *analogous practice*. Analogous practice might result from slight modifications in the nature of the instructional stimulus—for instance, the learner might be given practice exercises to do aloud rather than in writing. Or there might be slight modifications in the nature of the learner's response—he might be asked to respond in writing rather than aloud, or under slightly different time conditions. Both equivalent and analogues practice are excellent vehicles for helping the learner achieve an instructional objective.

A prime factor contributing to the presumptive effectiveness of appropriate practice is the frequency with which it is used. In general, we can assume that the more frequently a student has appropriate practice, the better.

Knowledge of Results.   According to the principle of knowledge of results, the student should be given an indication of whether his responses are correct. This information should be given as quickly as possibly, preferably during the same class period. Ideally, the student should know an instant after he makes a response whether it is appropriate or not. Therefore, teachers who systematically use this principle often devise practice tests in which the student makes responses and then finds out immediately afterward whether he is right or wrong. The students can exchange papers and correct each other's work, or the teacher can give the answers to practice questions—any method by which the student can determine whether his responses are right or wrong is acceptable. Even in dealing with students' responses to oral questions, the teacher should let the student know whether he is right or wrong. (This, of course, is almost impossible to avoid in normal discourse between student and teacher.)

How much delay can occur between the response and confirmation has not been determined. However, it is generally agreed that immediate confirmation is preferable to delayed confirmation. The presumptive-effectiveness criteria for this principle are (1) the immediacy with which the knowledge of results is given—that is, the sooner the student finds out, the better—and (2) the frequency with which the knowledge-of-results principle is used.

Some teachers put a one-hour time limit on themselves with respect to the use of knowledge of results. If knowledge of results has not been supplied within one hour after the student's response, then it is not technically considered to be knowledge of results. Obviously, if the learner does not find out what the results of his examination performance are until well after the examination is over, it does him far less good. On the other hand, even very delayed knowledge of results is better than no knowledge of results whatsoever.

Task Analysis
The teacher will discover that even though the instructional objectives may be stated in terms of desirable *terminal* behaviors of the learner—that is,

the behaviors the learner should be able to demonstrate at the close of instruction—there are a number of other behaviors that may be necessary in order for learners to achieve those terminal goals. These intermediate or sub-objectives are referred to as *en route behaviors*. The determination of these en route behaviors and the subsequent sequencing of such behaviors (that is, deciding which ones the learners will encounter first, second, third, and so on) is one of the more difficult problems facing instructional specialists. Instructional psychologists who have worked with this problem have developed exotic laboratory procedures for approaching the task, but, for most classroom teachers, they have relatively modest advice to offer. About the best guidance they can give is the following: When you have determined a terminal instructional objective, ask yourself the question "What does the learner need to be able to do in order to display his behavior?" By considering what the learner needs to do first, you will characteristically discover a preliminary behavior. The question should then be asked again for each identified en route behavior. This forms a kind of backward analysis that should ultimately reach the point at which the student begins the instructional sequence.

Because the teacher is not anxious to undertake *all* instructional responsibilities from the very beginning of the child's learning life, there must be some behaviors the learner brings to the instructional program. These are referred to as *entry behaviors* and represent the abilities and prior achievements that the learner has when he commences the instructional sequence.

A task analysis, no matter how simple, will usually be of some assistance to a teacher in that it identifies (1) important en route behaviors for which the teacher is responsible, and (2) important entry behaviors for which the teacher bears no responsibility.

Written Plans

New teachers, in particular, are urged to describe their instructional plans in writing. Many experienced teachers also prefer to write out their instructional plans because they can frequently "write themselves clearheaded" regarding the nature of their instructional decisions. The two most popular forms of written instructional plans are the *teaching unit* and the *lesson plan*.

The Teaching Unit. The teaching unit is a plan of instruction which covers more than a single class period. A teaching unit could last only two or three days, or it could extend over an entire semester. Most teaching units, however, cover periods of several weeks. Although there are some variations regarding the necessary ingredients of the teaching unit, it is recommended that the following seven elements be included in all teaching units:

1. *Precise Instructional Objectives.* All instructional objectives for the time period under consideration should be given in precise, measurable form.
2. *Pre-Test.* The actual pre-test to be used in connection with the instructional unit should be included.
3. *Day-by-Day Activities.* The day-by-day activities for the unit should be described in brief paragraph form. They should not be written out in great detail, for temporal estimates may be in error.
4. *Criterion Check.* This is a type of "pre-final exam" and consists of a representative sample of the post-test. It is administered to the learners *before* the end of instruction so that if they are unable to master the criterion behaviors, there is still some time to do something about it. Usually, the criterion check is administered several days before the actual post-test is given.
5. *Post-Test.* A complete post-test covering all instructional objectives should be included.
6. *Resources.* Any important instructional aids, such as references and audio-visual materials, should be cited.
7. *Back-up Lesson.* It is recommended that a lesson plan be included for a single period so that if something unforeseen occurs—for example, if a film fails to arrive—the teacher will have some relevant lesson ready to throw into the vacuum. This use of a back-up lesson can offer the beginning teacher confidence by giving him something to fall back on.

Of course, there can be variations in the nature of teaching units. Many school districts prefer that they be organized around elements somewhat different from those described above. However, with minor modifications, a plan involving these seven elements should prove serviceable to the teacher.

Lesson Plans. Since the lesson plan is designed to cover only a single class period, it is obviously more detailed than the teaching unit, which must cover planning for a number of days. If the following five elements are included in a lesson plan, the teacher will find that most of the requisite ingredients are present:

1. *Precise Instructional Objectives.* The particular objectives to be covered during the class lesson are described. Sometimes these will be the same objectives for several days in a row, so the teacher may wish to refer to them simply as "Objective 5 in the teaching unit," "Objective 7 in the teaching unit," and so on.

2. *Learner Activities.* The teacher describes what the learners will be doing during the period—for example, discussing, completing particular kinds of research requirements, and so forth.

3. *Teacher Activities.* A description is given of what the teacher will be doing during the class session, such as lecturing or demonstrating.

4. *Time Estimates.* Minute-by-minute estimates are made regarding how long the various learner and teacher activities will take. For example, the teacher may plan to take approximately ten minutes in introducing a topic—this time should be estimated even though the actual explanation may take somewhat longer. These estimates are only approximate, but they are better than nothing in guiding the teacher's planned use of the available minutes.

5. *Assignments (If Any).* If any assignments are to be given to the students, they should be identified in the lesson plan along with their due dates.

A suggested form for a lesson plan is included in Part 9 (page 105). This form incorporates all of the features described here.

Teacher-Directed Instructional Techniques

Even though it is unfortunate that so many teachers are evaluated exclusively on the basis of how they appear to be running their classrooms, it is undoubtedly true that certain teacher mannerisms do affect the quality of learning. For example, if a teacher has a series of disconcerting speech habits, even the most ingeniously devised instructional plan may be harmed by these distracting qualities. Thus there is some value in considering such factors as the way a teacher lectures, leads discussions, and gives demonstrations.

Over the years many writers have suggested rules of thumb regarding the ways in which lecturing, demonstrating, discussion leading, and questioning can be best conducted by the teacher. These rules are more experienced-based than experimentally verified and, as such, are offered here with some reservations. Surely, after reading these simple rules, a teacher will not instantly be able to incorporate them. For instance, it might be necessary for a teacher to take a systematic public speaking course in order to increase his lecturing proficiency. However, an examination of the rules may call any habitual violation to the teacher's attention and it may give him some cues regarding errors to be avoided. Accordingly, the following rules, from a number of writers, are offered:

Lecturing
1. Plan the content of the lecture in advance.
2. Do not speak too rapidly.
3. Employ verbal enthusiasm, speaking somewhat louder than you think necessary.
4. Use a conversational speaking style, maintaining frequent eye contact.
5. Use short sentences and simple language.
6. Explain new words.
7. Modify your presentation according to student reaction.
8. Employ humorous illustrations adding to the clarification of your ideas.
9. Move freely in front of the class but guard against undesirable habits.
10. Ask questions.
11. Always summarize.

Demonstrating
1. In general, demonstrating is most effective for teaching scientific principles and theories, movement or relationship of parts of tools and equipment, and manipulative operations.
2. Give demonstrations when a few advanced students are ready (either to the entire group or to sub-groups).
3. Plan the demonstrations carefully to ensure that all the requisite equipment is available.
4. Make certain that all of the students can see the demonstration.

5. If several methods of performing an operation are available, be sure to teach one method thoroughly before you introduce other methods.
6. Make certain that you can perform the skill to be demonstrated.
7. After each part or major step of the demonstration, ask questions to make sure that you are being understood.
8. Provide follow-up, or student application, after each demonstration.
9. In the demonstration of potentially dangerous equipment, emphasize safety precautions.

Leading a Discussion

1. Discussion questions typically involve the process of evaluation.
2. Use discussions for questions that are important enough to deserve the time that discussions take.
3. Make sure that your students are sufficiently informed on the topic of the discussion.
4. Prepare for class discussion in advance.
5. Center discussions around problems that the students recognize as important.
6. Help your students develop skill in discussion techniques.
7. Keep the discussion from rambling by making sure that students understand the problem.
8. In general, avoid following up tangential remarks in preference to the topic at hand.
9. At the close of the discussion summarize the major points discussed and conclusions reached.

Questioning

1. A good question should be easily understood, thought provoking, and on the main points of the lesson.
2. Address questions to the whole class.
3. Do not repeat questions that have been clearly presented.
4. As a general rule, do not repeat the students' answers.
5. Plan questions in a purposeful order.
6. When students give no answer to a question, substitute for the difficult question one of its component parts.
7. When a student gives an unimportant or incorrect answer, treat his response tactfully.

8. Stress significant answers.

9. If a student's response has been ungrammatically expressed, gauge your response according to the gravity of the error.

Discipline

Another topic related to effective instructional procedures has to do with discipline or classroom control. Educational researchers are beginning to attend to discipline with some degree of experimental rigor. We are now beginning to get some cues as to how a teacher should behave toward specific discipline problems in particular situations. Yet our knowledge of this important subject is far from adequate. Accordingly, the best that can be offered currently is a collection of experienced-based general principles and specific techniques that may be of use in guiding the teacher's responses to disciplinary difficulties. For the moment, the area of discipline is one in which the teacher will have to experiment to find out which general rules and specific techniques work best in his own classroom.

General Principles.   The six general principles that follow should guide the teacher's overall discipline strategy:

1. *Develop an Exciting Learning Program.* Generally speaking, most disciplinary problems arise when there is something deficient about the quality of the learning program. The teacher ought to consider the frequent occurrence of disciplinary difficulties as a clear indication of inadequacies in the instructional sequence. He should look immediately to the quality of the instructional program and try to make it more stimulating, rather than judging the students as the culprits in the situation.

2. *Diagnose the Cause.* Sometimes we are obliged to treat the symptom of a physical ailment without knowing the cause of that symptom. For example, physicians treat cancer even though its cause is not completely known. On the other hand, if somebody has a pain in his side caused by appendicitis, his treatment should not consist only of aspirin to deaden the pain. A skillful physician is not primarily concerned with eliminating symptoms, but rather with diagnosing the cause of those symptoms. Similarly, a teacher who is confronted with a destructive or disturbing classroom event should consider that event to be a symptom of an underlying

cause and should attempt to diagnose the cause of the disciplinary problem rather than treat the superficial aspects of the situation.

3. *Consider the Students' Backgrounds.* There is some modest empirical evidence that the more a teacher knows about his students, the better the level of order that will be maintained in his classroom. Perhaps this is because the student feels that he is dealing with a teacher who really knows him, or because the teacher can make more skillful decisions on the basis of his knowledge of the pupil. Whatever the reason, the evidence does suggest that the more teachers know about the backgrounds of their learners, the better their classroom disciplinary situation will be.

4. *Anticipate Disciplinary Problems.* A number of writers refer to the importance of anticipating disciplinary difficulties. For example, when a student takes out a piece of paper and begins to wad it up, strumming a rubber band at the same time, he is not necessarily practicing for next period's music class. The teacher should be attentive to such preliminary cues and should try to eliminate the difficulty before it turns into a significant (and possibly painful) incident.

5. *Discipline with Conviction.* Even though some of the rules established in a school may be difficult for the teacher to support totally, those rules ought to be enforced with a degree of conviction that suggests to the students that the teacher really wishes them to behave in particular ways. It is very difficult for a student to obey particular rules when the teacher enforces them with only modest conviction.

6. *Keep Procedures Consistent.* A student is easily confused when some rules are enforced while others are not, and when still other rules are enforced only occasionally. It is clearly desirable to be consistent in enforcing all disciplinary rules. The teacher should communicate the limits to the students and enforce those limits with great consistency.

Specific Techniques. The following fifteen specific disciplinary techniques have been described by several writers, notably Redl and Wattenberg.[5] The teacher may wish to try out these techniques to see which ones prove serviceable for him.

---

[5]F. Redl and W.W. Wattenberg, *Mental Hygiene in Teaching* (New York: Harcourt, Brace & World, 1951).

1. *Signal Interference.* A trick most teachers have learned is to catch the eye of a student who is beginning to get into mischief. The teacher then flashes a mildly disapproving warning by some signal such as nodding his head, frowning, waving a finger, or clearing his throat, and this signal is all that is needed. It calls attention to the fact that what is going on should be controlled. After receiving the signal, the pupil does the controlling by his own volition.

2. *Proximity Control.* A rather similar technique is employed on the many occasions when students are tempted to do something they know they should not do. If the teacher moves close to them, they will be better able to control their impulses. This works not so much because they fear detection as because they draw added strength from the teacher's nearness. Many teachers recognize this mechanism and use it wisely by placing a youngster with weak self-control in a seat close to the desk the teacher usually occupies.

3. *Humor to Relieve Tensions.* Laughter can serve several useful functions. When a youngster is engaging in undesirable conduct through thoughtlessness or for other minor reasons, a benign joke may call his attention to the lapse. At the same time, the humor reassures him that he has no immediate cause for anxiety.

4. *Planful Ignoring.* Under some conditions, deliberately ignoring the misbehavior—with disapproval tacitly implied—enables a student to reduce the inner tensions driving him to create disturbances. Before using this technique, however, the teacher must ask himself two basic questions: "Will the wrongdoer go on to other, more flagrant behavior to precipitate a scene?" "Will the behavior spread to other members of the class?" If the answer to both questions is "No," it may be wise to do nothing for the moment. When a young person gets no response from his attempt to get a rise from the teacher, he frequently stops the undesirable behavior.

5. *Gripe Sessions.* Many incidents involving annoying classroom conduct arise because one or more of the students is dissatisfied with some aspect of school or group life. Not knowing what to do about their feeling, such students engage in rebellious, aggressive behavior, or they lose interest in the work. It is important to realize that, for the participants, real benefits come from being able to express freely how they feel. The

teacher's proper role is to encourage honest discussion of student complaints and to help the young people express themselves.

6. *Helping Students Over Hurdles.* Much disorder in the schools arises because youngsters do not know how to cope with some phase of the work. For example, members of a high-school class committee may engage in random mischief if they lack the know-how to bring together individual findings into a group report. By helping young people over such hurdles, a teacher can save them from frustration and anxiety and thus eliminate inappropriate behavior.

7. *Restructuring the Situation.* One problem that sometimes arises is that students grow restless because they have been sitting still too long. In some cases it may be wise to change the nature of the activity or to give the group a new center for attention.

8. *Support from Routines.* In some groups, trouble arises because the young people cannot manage themselves in situations where they do not know what is expected of them. In order to check impulses that could lead to trouble, they need some support in the form of expectations they must meet. The establishment of a group pattern of doing things meets this need.

9. *Painless Removal.* Sometimes events may take such a turn that the behavior of a group hampers a youngster's ability to control himself. He may have a fit of giggling, for example. On such occasion, the child must be removed for his own good as well as for the order of the class. The adjective "painless" is used here to indicate that such removal is not to be considered punishment.

10. *Use of Restraint.* Now and then a child's actions threaten to harm other members of the group. In such emergencies, the child must be physically restrained; there is no alternative. There is no implication here of punishment; the restraint has to be entirely a protective action.

11. *Direct Appeal.* Behavior in the classroom may often be guided by simply asking the students to be good. For instance, a noisy room may be quieted by pointing out that no one can hear what anyone else is saying.

12. *Teacher-Conducted Analysis of Student Action.* Another common disciplinary device is a teacher-conducted analysis of a student's actions. This may be done either in private or within the hearing of the entire

class. We are not referring to scoldings or to tirades designed to inspire fear or create embarrassment. Rather, we are discussing those efforts, usually made in a helpful spirit, to give a student or a group greater insight into the adequacy of their conduct.

13. *Defining Limits.* Sometimes, when students misbehave, they are trying to determine the limits on their behavior. In some cases, the limit is simple enough that the teacher can prevent needless turmoil merely by forbidding or permitting an action (for example, declaring that there shall be no gum chewing).

14. *Post-Situational Follow-Up.* The meanings attached to a particular incident often require some time to take shape in the participants' minds. Immediately after something has happened, emotions may be so strong that rational thinking is difficult. However, after the excitement has abated, the teacher can explain to an individual or group the reasons that certain action was necessary.

15. *Marginal Use of Interpretation.* As has been mentioned often, a student's conduct may spring from motives he does not understand. Occasionally, in a classroom situation, a student can gain control over his actions by being given some insight into their meaning.

Instructional Decision Making

Even when he is following all of the above prescriptions, the teacher should bear in mind that instructional decisions may subsequently prove to be inadequate. The empirical evidence regarding the adequacy of these decisions is based, of course, on the criterion of what happens to the learner.

EVALUATION

The final component of our criterion-referenced instructional paradigm is evaluation. The term *evaluation*, as it is used in this book, refers to an assessment of the quality of the teacher's curricular and instructional decisions. It is the responsibility of the instructor to see that the objectives he originally formulated have been achieved. If they have, he can congratulate himself on a successful instructional sequence, and he should attempt to accomplish higher-level or additional objectives the next time he teaches the same or a comparable instructional sequence. If he has been unsuccessful, he must restructure the instructional procedure or his original curricular decisions.

When objectives are not achieved at the close of an instructional sequence, there are two principal explanations. First, the instruction might have been deficient. Second, the objectives might have been beyond the reach of the learners. Although the second explanation is possible, the teacher should consider the first—that is, ineffective instruction—as the most likely contender. Only after several unsuccessful attempts to accomplish given instructional objectives should the teacher really reconsider whether the objectives are too advanced for the students. Obviously, it is far easier to assert that the objectives are beyond the reach of the students than to revise an instructional sequence. This tendency should be counteracted by first looking to deficiencies in the instructional sequence. But even if the objectives *are* achieved, the teacher should once more consider the quality of his curricular decisions. He may be able to promote even more worthwhile objectives.

This conception of evaluation is essentially an outcome-oriented approach to evaluation because it is focused primarily on whether or not a pre-specified criterion has been achieved. There are many advocates of a more comprehensive conception of evaluation, in which the evaluator would supply information useful to educational decision makers at all points in the instructional process, from curriculum to final judgment of instructional outcomes. The merits of one such information–decision-making model will be compared with those of the outcome-oriented model proposed here.

Formative and Summative Evaluation.   Formative evaluation concerns the judgment of the quality of an instructional sequence while it is still in the development stages. For example, when a teacher develops an instructional unit and tries it out for the first time with a view to discovering its strengths and weaknesses, he may be considered to be engaging in formative evaluation. He evaluates for purposes of improvement. Summative evaluation involves a final comparison among competing instructional sequences. For example, if an instructor has an instructional sequence polished to his satisfaction, he might wish to compare it against an alternative instructional sequence to see which was more effective.

With respect to these kinds of comparisons, particularly those made in formative evaluation, most teachers will say that they teach innumerable lessons, many only once a year. For example, a high school teacher with five different classes may teach a given lesson on local government only in the fall term of each year. Thus, attempts to revise and improve the quality of that particular instructional sequence may be directed toward a lesson that will not recur for many months. The teacher must therefore apply improvement procedures either to lessons he teaches several times (if he teaches several classes in the same subject) or, more frequently, to certain elements that are common to a number of different lessons. For example, perhaps the lesson on local government in the previous example might be comparable to other lessons on national government or even somewhat less related topics. Generalizations regarding instructional tactics can be applied to instructional situations having comparable elements.

Measurement Considerations

An important difference between two distinctive approaches to measurement is emphasized by measurement specialists. This distinction compares (1) a classical approach to measurement, designed to compare individuals with one another, and (2) a more recent conception of measurement, designed to compare individuals with a given performance standard.

Norm-Referenced Measurement. Norm-referenced measurement is designed to contrast an individual's performance on a measuring device with the performance of other individuals on that same device. Standardized tests have classically been devised to "spread people out" so that one could assert, for example, that Johnny Harris scored at the eighty-third percentile —that is, he exceeded the performance of essentially 83 percent of those who took the test. These standardized tests have historically been developed with scores interpreted in reference to some norm group. In preparing, improving, and revising test items for such examinations, it is necessary that the items produce variant scores—different individuals must tend to get different scores so that they can be contrasted.

Criterion-Referenced Measurement. Criterion-referenced measurement is designed to compare an individual with a given performance standard, irrespective of how other individuals perform on the same test. For instance, a person must reach a given level of proficiency on the Red Cross Senior Lifesaving Test in order to pass the examination—regardless of how well or how poorly others perform on that test.

In situations where selectivity is required—where only a proportion of the individuals under consideration have a possibility of being selected for an advanced program, for example—then norm-referenced approaches are highly appropriate. In a situation where we wish to judge the quality of our instruction, however, as would be the case in the use of our empirically oriented instructional paradigm, then criterion-referenced measurement is in order. A teacher need not become involved with the complexities of this topic, although those interested may refer to more extensive treatments of the subject.[6] The important point to note, however, is that certain procedures that have been revered by measurement specialists through the decades should not be employed in connection with the assessment of the quality of an instructional sequence. For example, a test item which everyone answers incorrectly before instruction and which everyone answers correctly after instruction would usually be rejected by norm-referenced measurement specialists because it produces no variability in the post-test performance of the learners. Used to judge the quality of an instructional sequence, however, the item is perfectly suitable.

It is important to note in connection with criterion-referenced measurement that whereas we are attempting to produce *reliable* tests—that is, tests that measure the attainment of objectives with a great deal of consistency—the kind of *validity* we are most concerned with is referred to as *content validity*. Content validity is based on the judgment of experts regarding the congruence between test items and the objectives they are designed to measure. Content validity, as indicated, is therefore a judgmental operation and is, of course, greatly facilitated through the use of explicitly stated measurable objectives.

Classes of Criterion Measures

Unfortunately, many teachers think only of using standard paper-and-pencil measures when they attempt to assess instructional objectives. Indeed, their

---

[6]W.J. Popham and T.R. Husek, "Implications of Criterion-Referenced Measurement," *Journal of Educational Measurement* 6 (Spring 1969): 1–9.

conception of potential instructional objectives is sometimes limited by their restricted notion of what might serve as an acceptable criterion measure. One useful approach to generating diverse kinds of criterion measures is to classify such measures according to two dimensions: (1) whether the measurement is based on responses to *natural or manipulated stimulus conditions* and (2) whether the measurement involves *learner behavior or learner product*. The distinction between product and behavior is rather straightforward. If the outcome of an instructional sequence results in some kind of learner product—that is, a tangible object that may be subsequently scrutinized—then the criterion measure can be considered to yield a product. If, on the other hand, the learner shows that he has achieved the objective by displaying some kind of behavior (with no tangible product resulting), then we are clearly dealing with learner behavior rather than with a product. When a student writes an essay in an English class, for example, completes a written test in a history class, we have examples of learner products. When, on the other hand, the student gives a speech in a public speaking class or runs the hundred-yard dash in a physical education class, he has produced no tangible product and we should regard these activities as instances of pupil behavior. If it is *necessary* for an evaluator to *record* the learner's response, invariably a learner behavior rather than a product is involved.

Both learner products and behaviors can be also distinguished on the basis of whether they occur in response to natural (everyday) stimulus conditions or whether the teacher deliberately manipulates (contrives) stimulus conditions in order to see how learners will behave. For example, almost all formal test situations are examples of manipulated stimulus conditions. But there may be some intriguing situations in which we are interested to see how the learner will behave when he is not aware of how he "should" behave. Particularly in the affective domain there may be instances where we are anxious to see how the learner will respond when he is essentially uncued, when he has no idea of how he is expected to behave and might, therefore, behave in a more natural fashion. Examples of each of these four classes of criterion measures are given below in order to illustrate the classification system.

Learner Behavior—Manipulated Conditions. A drama teacher sets up one-act plays for his class and records the degree to which students follow his directions with respect to their gestures.

Learner Product—Manipulated Conditions. An English teacher directs her students to write three short paragraphs, each of which should have a clearly identifiable topic sentence.

Learner Behavior—Natural Conditions. An elementary teacher surreptitiously observes how her students behave during a recess period. She is anxious to note the degree to which they display courtesy toward their fellow students.

Learner Product—Natural Conditions. A junior high school faculty team inspects the amount of litter on the school grounds during the week before and the week after a special anti-litter campaign.

The reader should generate more examples like these in order to become more adept in the identification of measuring schemes.

Test Construction

The operations associated with designing, administering, and scoring a test are beyond the scope of this brief volume. Hopefully, most teachers will take some kind of formal test construction course to become familiar with the many nuances of testing. Unfortunately, most of the standard measurement tests reflect a norm-referenced rather than criterion-referenced approach to testing. Many recent books, for example, still urge the teacher to develop test items that will be answered correctly by only 50 percent of the class, for such items are designed to produce the most variability. Item-analysis techniques are recommended for identifying items that do not adequately discriminate between the less and the more knowledgeable students in the class, and the teacher is advised to discard such items. Unfortunately, these texts do not describe approaches to measurement that are of complete utility in a criterion-referenced instructional paradigm. Even so, they offer some valuable tips to the prospective item writer. For instance, a teacher will learn how to avoid designing test items with construction flaws that enable students to answer correctly when they really do not know what the items are measuring. If the teacher keeps in mind the important distinctions between norm-referenced and criterion-referenced measurement, most of these texts will be of some value to him.

Item Sampling

A scheme has recently been developed by measurement specialists to help the teacher assess the degree to which his instructional objectives have been effectively promoted. This scheme involves giving shorter tests to students and using different test forms for different pupils. Suppose that a teacher has three objectives, with four test items for each objective, for a two-week teaching unit. Instead of giving the entire class a twelve-item test, the teacher might, *if his only purpose is to assess his instructional proficiency,* administer a different four-item test to each quarter of his class. Each of the tests might contain one item measuring each of the four objectives, but the item would be stated in a different way on each of the four forms. The teacher could distribute these tests randomly among the class and thus get a reasonably good idea of the proportion of the class that has mastered each objective.

If grades are to be assigned on the basis of a test, it is necessary to have all students complete the same (or a comparable) test form. But there are many instances in which a teacher can, even by giving a *single item* to each of his pupils (if different items are given to different pupils), judge the quality of an instructional sequence.

Grading

In most teaching situations, an instructor is faced with the responsibility of assigning grades to pupils. This is a harrowing experience to a new teacher, and only the benefit of advanced years makes the job less distressing for a seasoned teacher. Grading is a largely subjective, extremely imprecise operation which, unfortunately, most teachers must carry out.

Recognizing that this is the case, the teacher should certainly be aware of the fact that an effective instructional sequence, systematically improved over a period of time through the use of a criterion-referenced approach, will very likely produce higher performance for more learners. This being the case, the teacher should feel no qualms whatsoever about giving a higher proportion of excellent grades than he did before he adopted a criterion-referenced strategy. Some teachers erroneously assume that unless they give a certain number of low grades, their standards are too lenient. What we should really like to occur in education is for almost all of our pupils to receive grades of A and B, with very few students receiving low grades.

Realistic expectations of children, unfortunately, preclude the probability that all of them will get A's. There may be a few students who, no matter how effective the instructional sequence, will not be responsive, and the teacher will therefore have to give them, low grades. But, in such cases, leniency is urged. Since grading is usually so imprecise, borderline cases should generally be given the benefit of the doubt. Because of this imprecision, the teacher should derive some solace by realizing that even if he erroneously penalizes a student by awarding him an unfairly low grade, chances are that over the entire period of the youngster's educational experience he is likely to be benefitted as often as he is penalized. In other words, one teacher's grading error will probably be compensated for by another teacher's mistake in the opposite direction. It is small consolation, but in this area teachers should escape as much guilt as possible.

Assessing the Quality of Teaching

There will be efforts during a teacher's career to judge the quality of his instructional efforts. Supervisors will be in a position to make a judgment regarding how well the teacher actually instructs. Although the beginning teacher usually cannot modify the evaluation system completely (even an experienced teacher will have some difficulty in doing this), it is recommended that any scheme designed to evaluate the teacher's proficiency should be predicated in large measure on that teacher's ability to modify the behavior of the learners.

Too often a supervisor will judge a teacher primarily on the basis of whether that teacher employs the instructional techniques that the supervisor used during his own (stellar) days as a classroom teacher. If the teacher lectures in the same way that the supervisor lectured, he will probably be considered a good teacher. If he behaves differently, he is likely to be considered deficient.

We have sufficient experimental evidence to demonstrate graphically that there is no single set of instructional procedures that *invariably* produce learner growth. For different teachers, different objectives, and different pupils, the use of a variety of diverse instructional procedures may be effective. What works well for one teacher may be anathema to another. This being the case, what we really have to focus on in judging the quality of the teacher is *the degree to which he can promote desirable behavior changes in learners.*

A supervisor should engage in two primary activities with a teacher. First, he should attempt to improve the quality of the instructional objectives that the teacher selects, to ensure that those objectives represent the most worthwhile goals that can be sought for the pupils under consideration. Second, he should help the teacher devise improved methods of accomplishing those goals. Instructional variations should be tried out much like hypotheses. The teacher should be encouraged to test the adequacy of alternative instructional tactics. But once the teacher has achieved worthwhile goals—in spite of whether the evaluator thinks the teacher is behaving in the classroom in the way he thinks the "good" teacher ought to behave—the teacher should be judged proficient.

The criterion-referenced instructional model described here is designed to improve the teacher's instructional decision making so that, using the criterion of learner growth, the teacher can be properly designated as a truly effective instructor.

Part 4

Sample Test Items

Each of the instructional objectives in Part 1 is represented in this section by a sample test item. The items are identified by the topic (curriculum, instruction, or evaluation) and by the objective number. For example, sample item E-2 is based on the second objective in the list of evaluation objectives.

CURRICULUM

C- 1. *Measurable Objectives.* From the set of educational objectives given below, identify any which are stated in terms of measurable student behavior by placing an X before the objective.

_____ The student will learn the important elements of Shakespearean drama.

_____ The student will name, in writing, all of the Shakespearean tragedies.

_____ The student will appreciate, at the end of the course, the beauty of Shakespearean sonnets.

C- 2. *Writing Objectives.* Write at least two behaviorally stated objectives for the following broad goal: "Pupils will learn about everyday life in Norway."

C- 3. *Content Generality.* Identify, by marking it with an X, any of the following objectives which possesses content generality rather than test-item equivalence.

_____ Presented with any poem from Romantic period which was not previously treated in class, the pupil can name the poet.

_____ The pupil can correctly add at least 80 percent of twenty pairs of triple-digit numbers randomly generated by the teacher.

_____ The student can name aloud seven of the ten most recent presidents of the United States.

C- 4. *Performance Standards.* For the following objectives, circle the S if the objective has only a *student* minimal level of learner behavior; circle the C if the objective has a *class* minimal level of learner behavior; circle the N if the objective has *no* minimal level of learner behavior.

S C N The students will paint a still-life study employing two-point perspective and at least three colors.

S C N Everyone in class will orally recite a given Spanish dialogue with no errors in pronunciation.

S C N Students will be able to match chemical compounds with their valences on a written test.

C- 5. *Objective Domains.* Indicate which objective domain the following activity best fits: "The pupil will be able to type at least thirty-five words per minute." This objective is primarily

a. affective
b. psychomotor
c. cognitive—lowest level
d. cognitive—higher than lowest level

C- 6. *Taxonomic Level.* Indicate the best taxonomic level for classifying the following objective: "The pupil can discriminate among previously unencountered essays according to which most accurately reflects specified criteria of style."

a. knowledge
b. valuing
c. evaluation
d. responding

C- 7. *Generating Objectives.* For the following non-behavioral objective, list as many measurable objectives as you can which accurately reflect that objective: "The learner will become more interested in the course subject matter."

C- 8. *End and Means.* Check those questions below that are more relevant to instructional *ends* than to instructional *means.*

_____ What should be taught in class?

_____ Will textbook X be more effective than textbook Y?

_____ How much time should be devoted to classroom discussion?

C- 9. *Tyler Rationale.* In the space provided, give the name of one of the seven components of Tyler's curricular rationale which best describes each of the following operations.

_____ Consulting academic experts regarding what should be taught.

_____ Deciding what objectives can be realistically accomplished in the available time.

C-10. *Preassessment.* Which of the following teachers is making the best use of preassessment data?

a. Teacher X discovers from her pre-test that two of her thirty-five pupils cannot master one of her ten objectives for the unit on local government. Because all ten objectives are very important, she decides to cover all ten goals for the entire class.

b. Teacher Y encounters a situation similar to Teacher X's, but she decides to delete the one objective mastered by thirty-three of her pupils and to provide special make-up assignments for the two students who have not yet achieved that goal.

C-11. *Curriculum Terminology.* Learner behavior considered to be primarily of an intellectual nature is considered

a. cognitive

b. affective

c. psychomotor

INSTRUCTION

I- 1. *Instructional Principles.* For the following item, select the principle, if any, which the teacher clearly attempts to incorporate in the instructional activity. (It is possible that no principle should be selected.)

A French teacher introduces a unit on French idioms by presenting the class with a series of ten English idioms, each of which, understood as a whole, clearly has a meaning different from the joined meanings of its component parts. Having given an idiom such as "What's up?", she then points out its meaning. She deliberately chooses idioms that are difficult for her class to interpret. She observes that people who are unfamiliar with our language are often confused by such expressions and that the students should learn French idioms in order to communicate more effectively in French. The remainder of the period is devoted to the teacher's listing twenty-five common French idioms, accompanied by the English translations, on the board. Students are instructed to copy the material from the board and to be prepared to take a brief quiz on the idioms during the next class period. The teacher tells the students that the quiz will be worth twenty-five points in their nine-week grades.

a. revelation of objectives
b. perceived purpose
c. appropriate practice
d. knowledge of results

I- 2. *Effective Instructional Principles.* A learning principle is presented along with descriptions of three teachers' actions. Select the teacher who is, presumably, utilizing the principle most effectively. The principle is *appropriate practice.*

a. Government Teacher A's objective is to have his class critically evaluate published opinions on national and local issues. He believes that this will reflect the student's ability to distinguish those segments of a statement which are propagandistic from those segments which are properly supported by evidence. He has his class spend at least one day a week discussing the newspaper editorials he brings to class; these editorials often contain propagandistic material. After the class discussion, each member of the class must write a brief summary of the valid and invalid points contained in the editorials.

b. Government Teacher B has the same objective. Students are instructed to bring controversial editorials to class each Thursday, and most of the time they select materials that satisfy this requirement. Five students are chosen by the instructor to read their reports aloud. After each report, the instructor, and the class, try to repudiate the point of view taken by the editorial writer—preferably by non-propagandistic methods, although this is not required.

c. With the same objective, Government Teacher C reads extensive excerpts from propagandistic material produced in Germany during World War II. He attempts to analyze this material in such a way that the editorial techniques employed by the propagandist become clear to the students.

I- 3. *Teaching Assignments.*   Design a ten-minute lesson to teach three of your classmates. Prepare a lesson plan which incorporates the four instructional principles and carry out the lesson. An observer will determine the degree to which your plan and the actual lesson incorporate each principle. See the Observation Form in Part 9 (page 106).

I- 4. *Instructional Techniques.*   Select the teacher not violating one of the rules typically given for the instructional technique the teacher is using. The instructional technique is *lecturing.*

a. Teacher A devotes considerable attention to his twelfth-grade history class lectures. He plans the content of a particular day's lecture well in advance, making certain to incorporate appropriate illustrative material to describe the concepts he is treating. He has carefully studied the oratorical styles of great speakers of the past and he attempts to use these styles when he presents his topic. He centers the speaker's rostrum at the front of the class and, in an extremely eloquent and formal style, delivers his daily lectures.

b. Teacher B considers the lecture to be a method of communicating with students that is more effective when it is spontaneous. As a result, he rarely plans his history lectures in advance; instead, he attempts to lecture on a few main points. This results in a highly conversational, almost "chatty" lecture style. Teacher B moves freely in front of the class to further convey the impression of informality.

c. Teacher C prepares his history lectures in advance, but he delivers them in a markedly less formal fashion than History Teacher A. He speaks to his class as though he were communicating with the individual students, although in a somewhat louder voice than he would ordinarily use in normal conversation. Teacher C has excellent eye contact with his pupils during the lectures.

I- 5. *Teaching Units.* List and briefly describe the recommended elements that should be included in a teaching unit.

I- 6. *Lesson Plans.* List and briefly describe the recommended elements that should be included in a lesson plan.

I- 7. *Instructional Plans.* In the following question, an operational statement is made. Indicate, by circling the letter of the correct answer, whether this operation should be carried out in the preparation of teaching units, lesson plans, both, or neither. The operational statement: "A post-test is always included."

    a. teaching units
    b. lesson plans
    c. both
    d. neither

I- 8. *Discipline.* Mrs. Harris finds that one of her fourth-grade youngsters constantly causes disruptions by talking with other children during class activities. List at least four general principles and at least ten specific techniques that Mrs. Harris might use in dealing with this pupil.

I- 9. *Instructional Terminology.* The learner's behavioral repertoire as he commences an instructional program is called

    a. en route behavior
    b. terminal behavior
    c. criterion behavior
    d. entry behavior

EVALUATION

E- 1. *Evaluative Decisions.* When most of his seventh-grade pupils fail to achieve the majority of his instructional objectives for a four-week social studies unit, the teacher should

    a. automatically assume that the objectives are too difficult for the learners

    b. reappraise the quality of his instructional activities

    c. consider that the pupils are not working hard enough

    d. get much tougher with the class, assigning lower grades in the future for such performance

E- 2. *Testing Procedures.* Check any of the following practices that would be generally approved by evaluation and measurement specialists.

    _____ A teacher constructs an essay test and then evolves criteria for judging student responses as he reads the first few papers.

    _____ All of the teacher's examinations are composed of true-false items.

    _____ A test item that adequately measures an instructional objective is answered correctly by all of the students on the final examination. It is discarded by the teacher because it does not discriminate among learners.

E- 3. *Criterion Measures.* Using the following four-category scheme of criterion measures, classify each of the items listed below by writing the appropriate letter in the space provided: (a) learner behavior—natural conditions, (b) learner behavior—manipulated conditions, (c) learner product—natural conditions, (d) learner product—manipulated conditions.

    _____ Scores on the Kuder test of vocational interest.

    _____ Instances of pupil misbehavior during recess periods.

    _____ Surreptitious observations of learner behavior in nationally distributed "situational stress" tests involving accomplices.

E- 4. *Writing Test Items.* Write three test items that are congruent with the following instructional objective: "The learner will be able to multiply correctly any pair of double-digit numbers, demonstrating this skill by selecting the right answer from three alternatives."

E- 5. *Criterion- and Norm-Referenced Measurement.* Identify by placing C or N before the item whether the following operation is more appropriate for criterion-referenced (C) or norm-referenced testing (N).

_____ The use of judges to determine the validity of test items, that is, the degree to which the items are consonant with the objectives.

E- 6. *Item Sampling.* Describe, step by step, the basic procedure for constituting tests by an item-sampling procedure. Briefly, why would such tests be used?

E- 7. *Grading.* Check any of the following grading practices that are consistent with a criterion-referenced approach to instruction.

_____ Mr. Philren invariably assigns grades according to the normal curve, making sure that he has approximately equal proportions of A and F grades.

_____ Miss Finn finds that so many of her students attain the course objectives that she is obliged to award 78 percent of her class with A grades.

E- 8. *Evaluation Terminology.* Measurement approaches designed to determine an individual's status with respect to a given performance standard are called.

a. criterion-referenced
b. norm-referenced
c. correlated
d. valid

Part 5

Practice Exercises

In this section, practice exercises are provided for all of the objectives listed in Part 1 of the book. After finishing the expository material in Part 3, the reader should be able to undertake these exercises and perform relatively well. The correct answers are given in Part 8 (page 101) and should be consulted on the completion of each exercise. As in the sample test items in Part 4, the practice exercises are identified by topic and objective number. Thus, C-2 exercises are related to the second curriculum objective. The line in front of each exercise may be used for an assignment date, that is, the date by which the exercise must be completed.

CURRICULUM

—— C- 1. *Measurable Objectives.* Directions: Place an X before any objective that is stated in terms of observable student behavior.

1. The student will grasp the significance of the Treaty of Versailles.
2. The student will have an attitude favorable to English grammar as indicated by his response to a questionnaire.
3. The student will know six verbs.
4. The student will learn the names of the common tools in a wood shop.
5. The teacher will list three major causes of the Civil War on the chalkboard.

6. The student will prefer cooking to sewing.

7. The student will be able to thread a sewing machine correctly.

8. The student will be able to develop a sense of the cultural unity of man.

___ C- 2. *Writing Objectives.*   Change each of the following objectives so that it is stated in terms of learner behavior.

1. The student will learn about the Civil War.

2. The class will understand labor-management relations.

___ C- 3. *Content Generality.*   Indicate which, if any, of the following objectives possess content generality.

1. The learner will be able to drive any automatic transmission car.

2. The learner will be able to recite the Pledge of Allegiance.

3. The learner will be able to describe in an essay the effects of the Point Four Program in post-war Europe.

4. The learner will be able to write a summary of any nineteenth-century English narrative poem.

5. The learner will be able to write the alphabet in cursive script.

6. The learner will be able to solve the equation $7 + 3x + 2y = 16 - 2x$.

7. The learner will be able to describe the three motives discussed in class for Hamlet's behavior.

8. The learner will be able to spell twenty-five words randomly selected from a list of the "Thousand Hardest Words To Spell."

9. The learner will be able to balance correctly any chemistry equation chosen from the fifty exercises at the end of the text.

10. The learner will be able to draw an apple with proper shading.

___ C- 4. *Performance Standards.*   For the following objectives, mark *S* if the objective has only a student minimal level of learner performance, C if the objective has a class minimal level of learner performance, and N if the objective has no minimal level of performance.

1. The students in the class will answer correctly ten out of twelve multiple-choice questions on the Roman Empire.
2. The students will compose essays about their summer vacations.
3. At least ten students in the class will sign up for a senior lifesaving course at the conclusion of a unit on water safety.
4. Seventy-five percent of the students will understand differential equations.
5. Students will recite with no more than one error Milton's sonnet "On His Blindness."
6. Sixty percent of the students will prepare five-hundred-word reports on famous social scientists.
7. The students will thoroughly comprehend at least 80 percent of the scientific theories treated in class.
8. The students will paint still-life studies employing two-point perspective and at least three colors.
9. Everyone in class will recite a given Spanish dialogue with no errors in pronunciation.
10. Students will be able to match chemical compounds with their valences on a written test.

____ C- 5. *Objective Domains.* Classify the following objectives by marking the letter of the appropriate objective domain. The domains are (a) psychomotor, (b) affective, (c) cognitive —higher than lowest level, and (d) cognitive—lowest level.

1. The learner is able to choose the best of four solutions to a physics problem on linear acceleration, using formulas found in the book.
2. The learner exhibits concern for others by enrolling in the Peace Corps.
3. The learner lists the names and two traits of eight common mental disorders discussed in class.

4. The learner properly sews a three-piece suit.

5. The learner scores well on the Strong Vocational Interest Inventory.

6. The learner employs grammatical usages correctly in constructing term papers.

7. The learner plays tennis well enough to beat three amateurs 80 percent of the time.

8. The learner scores 75 percent or better on a vocabulary matching quiz.

9. The learner displays interest in books by reading in his spare time.

10. The learner plays the guitar technically as well as Montoya.

___ C- 6. *Taxonomic Level.* Select the category that is most appropriate for each objective.

1. When presented with pictures of children suffering from deficiency diseases, the student will be able to identify the particular disease on the basis of the symptoms.

a. comprehension
b. evaluation
c. synthesis
d. characterization

2. When given a novel set of specifications, the student will be able to design a building.

a. responding
b. analysis
c. synthesis
d. evaluation

3. As a leader of a discussion group, the student will demonstrate his belief in the worth of everybody's opinion by tactfully drawing out reticent group members.

a. comprehension
b. valuing
c. organization
d. attending

    4. The student will be able to state in words material presented in three different kinds of graphs.

       a. comprehension

       b. analysis

       c. knowledge

       d. organization

    5. The student will obey the playground instructions.

       a. knowledge

       b. comprehension

       c. responding

       d. application

___ C- 7. *Generating Objectives.* For the following general objective, write out as many behaviorally stated objectives as you can that reflect achievement of the general objective: "The student will display good sportsmanship."

___ C- 8. *Ends and Means.* Check any of the following items that indicate a change in educational *means* as opposed to *ends.*

    1. Adding new goals dealing with the southwestern U.S. to the history course.

    2. Reducing the number of skills developed in the English course in order to add more objectives covering the pupils' basic usage deficiencies.

    3. Rearranging the sequence of objectives treated in the physics course.

    4. Using new self-study pamphlets to teach current math topics.

    5. Dropping biology course objectives dealing with sex education.

___ C- 9. *Tyler Rationale.* Mark the letter of the Tyler Rationale component most closely associated with each of the phrases presented below. The Tyler Rationale components are (a) the student as a source, (b) the society as a source, (c) the subject as a source, (d) tentative objectives, (e) the philosophical screen, (f) the psychological screen, and (g) final objectives.

1. theories of motivation
2. pupil's hobbies
3. National Council of Teachers of English
4. vocations most in need of personnel
5. community survey on educational goal preferences
6. teacher's view of life
7. positive reinforcement
8. measurable behavior
9. personal information sheet prepared by the learner
10. imprecise goals

____ C-10. *Preassessment.* For the following two items, descriptions of the actions of three teachers are presented. Select the teacher in each group who is most effectively preassessing.

1. a. Teacher A has among his objectives one that is of an attitudinal nature—namely, that his students like his class and subject matter. Evidence of this "liking" will come from the students' responses to questionnaires that are to be anonymously filled out at the end of the semester. On the first day of class, Teacher A asks those who think they like English to raise their hands. Since most of the class responds positively, Teacher A decides that he has a genial group.

   b. Teacher B also desires that his students like his class and the content treated in it. He plans to measure this in the same way as Teacher A. However, he asks the students to fill out the questionnaire the first day of class, being careful to put their names on their papers.

   c. Teacher C has the same objective and same criterion measure as Teachers A and B. On the first day of class he passes out the questionnaire and asks the students to fill it out anonymously. After collecting the questionnaires, the teacher tells the class why he likes English.

2. a. Teacher A is initiating a new unit in his history class. Much of the information and many of the concepts

are on a high intellectual level, far above what one would expect of the typical ninth grader. Before dealing with Social Darwinism, Teacher A chooses two or three students who represent the different ability levels in his classroom and asks them what they know about this broad social concept. On the basis of the students' responses, Teacher A decides to modify his objectives and gives less background material than he had planned.

b. Teacher B also plans to treat Social Darwinism in his ninth-grade class. Before beginning his unit, he prepares a detailed pre-test that includes items relevant to each of his objectives. After scoring the students' tests, Teacher B realizes that the changes indicated by the class performance are not practical, and so he teaches the unit as he originally planned it.

c. Teacher C is also teaching a unit that will deal with Social Darwinism. Since time is short, he will have to progress through the unit rapidly. Teacher C believes in pre-testing thoroughly, but because of the time limitation, he spends only one fifteen-minute period at the beginning of the unit questioning his students on their knowledge of Social Darwinism. He discovers that the students have a rather distorted view of this topic, and so he plans to give special emphasis to points that he normally would have treated more casually.

___ C-11. *Curriculum Terminology.*   Select the term or phrase that best matches the definition.

1. The range of content covered by a course is known as
   a. scope
   b. sequence
   c. syllabus
   d. subject

2. A collection of suggested instructional activities is called a

    a. teaching unit

    b. course of study

    c. resource unit

    d. syllabus

3. An indicator used to judge the quality of an instructional program is called

    a. a criterion

    b. psychomotor

    c. a rule

    d. the sequence

INSTRUCTION

____ I- 1. *Instructional Principles.*

PART A. The following exercises are useful as an en route behavior before practicing the eight exercises in Part B. Circle the letter of each example in which the teacher is clearly using the instructional principle in question.

1. *Principle: Revelation of Objectives*

    a. A third-grade teacher, Mrs. McGuffy, wants her students to improve their reading proficiency. She informs them at the beginning of the academic year that it will be their responsibility to read much more efficiently as a consequence of their year with her.

    b. Mr. Adam, a sixth-grade instructor, begins a unit of work in long division by giving his pupils examples of each of the different kinds of division problems they will be expected to solve at the conclusion of the teaching unit. He spends fifteen minutes with the students going over these exercises so that they understand exactly what they are supposed to do.

    c. In a senior high school social studies class, the teacher has gone to great trouble to isolate the kinds of post-instruction learner behaviors he is attempting to promote. He has listed these behaviors in a four-page document which he has circulated among his colleagues for their criticism. After several revisions, he decides that the document reflects his intentions, and he makes copies of it, which he distributes to students at the beginning of the academic year. As the year progresses, some of the students ask for clarification of the meanings of these objectives. Such clarification is always supplied by the instructor.

2. *Principle: Perceived Purpose*

a. A high school speech teacher begins every semester's class in persuasive speaking by playing records of Richard Nixon's most important public addresses. He urges the class to pay careful attention to the persuasion techniques used by the President. He suggests that the group consider the importance of public speaking to a person's future success in life.

b. A high school business instructor begins each unit of his bookkeeping course by describing to the class the actual applications of the methods they are studying. He calls upon his own experiences in the business world and constantly tries to impress his students with the real significance of the bookkeeping methods they are studying.

c. Mrs. Frascati, a home economics instructor, makes sure to begin each cooking unit by showing her students how to cook an exotic dish that features the particular foods under study. For example, when the class studies poultry, Mrs. Frascati personally prepares a large portion of chicken in wine so that each student may sample the dish. Even though the administration occasionally raises objections to the use of alcohol in these recipes, Mrs. Frascati continues to begin her units in this fashion.

3. *Principle: Appropriate Practice*

   a. A history teacher has his class recite facts pertaining to the Civil War. His students learn names of battlefields by rote and the significance of battles through discussion. He is very pleased with their progress during the semester.

   b. An English teacher wants his students to become effective letter writers. He discusses the requisites of a well-composed letter with respect to the salutation, body, and closing of the letter. He also discusses various types of personal letters, such as "newsy," "thank you," and "invitation" letters. Following his presentation, the teacher has the students choose names of other pupils in the class and write one letter of each type to the individual selected.

   c. Mr. Brinkley, a social studies teacher who loves current events, wants his students to be able to identify the national leaders of at least five nations of Africa. He has two or three students make oral reports regarding the recent history of these leaders. He then gives the class practice in choosing the leaders by arranging brief, non-graded quiz sessions, in which he first names the country and then asks the students to write the name of the national leader. He gives the correct answers immediately after each practice quiz.

4. *Principle: Knowledge of Results*

   a. A junior high school English instructor wishes her students to learn to write Japanese haiku poetry. She has everyone in the class prepare one poem at the beginning of the period, then calls on at least half the students, one at a time, to read their poems. Because students are usually uneasy about reading their poetry, she tries to find something nice to say after each student's reading.

   b. A history teacher gives his classes brief quizzes every

other day covering the significant facts treated during the previous two days. He has his students grade their own papers after he reads the answers aloud. Students then turn in their quizzes so that the teacher can record the grades.

c. A high school history teacher gives her students an essay examination concerning the main points of the topic just completed. After the students have finished their papers and the tests have been collected, the teacher briefly describes those concepts she feels were necessary for the students to incorporate into their essays. She grades the papers and returns them three days later.

PART B. The following eight exercises provide practice in determining which, if any, of four instructional principles a teacher clearly uses in his class. Select those principles which are definitely used by the instructor in each example. There may be more than one principle (or none) used in each example. The principles: (a) revelation of objectives, (b) perceived purpose, (c) appropriate practice, and (d) knowledge of results.

1. Mr. Farly, an economics instructor, wants his students to understand the ramifications of the law of supply and demand. He has prepared an excellent set of notes on this topic which carefully proceed from examples of simple application to extremely subtle implications of these economic principles. Through the years, Mr. Farly has carefully revised his lecture notes so that the complexity of the concepts he treats will increase in very small steps, much like programmed instruction.

At the outset of the unit on supply and demand, Mr. Farly spends more than six periods trying to make the students see the importance of this particular economic law. He tries to draw examples of its application from each student's background. For instance, he uses the ex-

perience of Johnny Miles, the son of a local grocer, to
illustrate several facets of the law. He concludes the introduction by giving the students a printed set of the
unit objectives with one sample item for each objective.

During the unit, Mr. Farly lectures primarily. But, on
three occasions he divides the class into four sub-groups
on the basis of intelligence and past achievement. While
the remainder of the class reads assignments from the
text, he gives a brief special lecture to each group. These
extra lectures are pitched at the intellectual level of the
sub-groups. The pupils seem to appreciate Mr. Farly's
special sub-group lectures.

2. Miss Torrance teaches women's physical education at
   Jacobs Junior High School. Her objective for the last
   weeks of the spring semester is to have her pupils become sufficiently proficient in playing tennis that they
   can play a complete set and derive satisfaction and enjoyment from their play. A final examination for the tennis
   unit consists of each girl playing at least one set under
   the observation of Miss Torrance. The teacher plans to
   observe the behavior of the girls systematically during
   and after the final play to see (1) if they can play the
   game well, and (2) if they manifest visible enjoyment
   of the tennis activity. Before allowing the girls to play,
   however, Miss Torrance spends a full week as follows:
   Monday, rules of the game; Tuesday, equipment; Wednes-
   day, the forehand; Thursday, the backhand; and Friday,
   the service. When the actual play starts, Miss Torrance
   attempts to have the girls concentrate first on the forehand, then the backhand, and finally the service.

   Most of the six-week unit is spent in actual play, with
   each girl playing every other girl in the class for at least
   a quarter of one period. Very few days on the courts are
   rained out, so the girls get considerable practice. Based
   on the girls' terminal performance, Miss Torrance is satisfied with her instructional methods.

3. Mr. Jones, an English teacher, wants his students to be able to communicate effectively with others. His class is currently engaged in studying the parts of speech, and he has his students analyze sentences at home. They then respond in class to questions he asks regarding certain words in the homework assignment. A typical class session sees students called upon at least once. Mr. Jones tries to have above-average students identify the part of speech for the more difficult words. On occasion, however, he tries to challenge certain of the less able youngsters by giving them a moderately difficult word.

Since he notes grades in his book for every response, the youngsters pay close attention to his questions and, evidently, complete their homework assignments regularly. After a student responds to his question, Mr. Jones immediately tells him if he is right. If he is wrong, he chooses another student, continuing until someone identifies the word correctly as a particular part of speech.

The class sessions are conducted with such joviality that the students do not appear to be excessively threatened or anxious over the questioning routine.

4. Mr. Gage, a history teacher, introduces a unit on the United Nations midway through the school year. His objective is to have the students understand certain weaknesses and strengths in the structure of the United Nations. Students reveal their accomplishment of this objective as follows: When given certain statements regarding structure, procedure, and policy, they correctly associate the statement with the United Nations or the League of Nations.

At the beginning of the unit, Mr. Gage has all class members bring to class at least one story from the daily newspaper which mentions the United Nations. These articles are described in brief oral reports by each pupil. Mr. Gage then summarizes the diverse concerns of the United Nations and points out how important such matters are to everyone in the class. He attempts to bring this point home by describing the role of the United Nations in the Middle East crises and showing how a full-scale war may have been averted by the efforts of the United Nations' officials.

He continues this introduction during the next class by observing that deficiencies in the legal and procedural structure of the previous world forums have led to their ineffectiveness. It is crucial, Mr. Gage states, to know which structural defects may exist in an organization like the United Nations so they may be corrected through the force of world public opinion.

He assigns three of the more able students in class to report the following day on the rise and fall of the League of Nations. Several of the pupils of below-average ability are asked to arrange with the school librarian to have a special collection of United Nations books and documents brought to the room for two weeks, along with any materials relevant to the League of Nations that the librarian can locate. After the students report on the League of Nations, Mr. Gage summarizes the key points in the major legal statements of the United Nations and the League of Nations. For the next several days, the class is asked during discussions to describe the major actions of the United Nations and the League of Nations. Mr. Gage calls on everyone in the class at least twice, attempting to direct the more simple questions at his less able students.

5. Miss C. Lany, a drama teacher, has her students prepare a number of one-act comedies which will be presented to the student body of their high school. Her objective is to have the class appreciate good theater. Each student is assigned a role in the first meeting. The directors, stage managers, and actors are chosen and instructed to fulfill their respective responsibilities (planning, props, line

learning, etc.) before the end of the week. At the next meeting the teacher has the actors read their lines, during which time she makes suggestions on ways to improve gestures and intonation. At the following session, each play is run through without scripts; however, the teacher still makes suggestions for improvement. Soon thereafter, a dress rehearsal is held and students are very excited. One leading lady has a severe case of stage fright and forgets her lines. Miss Lany manages to calm her and prompt her until she remembers her part. Opening night comes, the plays are presented and pronounced "laugh-riots" by the critic from the school newspaper.

6. An English teacher wants her students to be able to make out source cards for use in library research. On the day before a library period, she spends part of the class time explaining the proper procedures to be used in making out one of these cards. She also shows the class a diagram of the location of the card catalogue file and briefly comments on the Dewey Decimal System of cross-filing books. The next day the class proceeds to the library, where each student goes to the card file to determine the location of his book. Each pupil secures his book and spends the rest of the period reading. The next day the teacher passes out $5'' \times 7''$ cards so that students can make source cards. These cards are used by the teacher to measure the quality of her instruction.

7. Miss Dee Meenor plans to have her history students understand John Stuart Mill's essay "On Liberty." Miss Meenor first discusses the nature of independent thought and the relationship of the individual to the government. She asks her students to think of ways such a problem might be relevant today. Students mention activities of the ACLU, problems of the Rumford Act, and zoning restrictions. The teacher then notes that many men have worried about this problem for years. Mimeographed

copies of John Stuart Mill's "On Liberty" are passed out and students spend the remainder of the class period reading this essay.

8. Mr. Rees F. Nature wants students in his life science class to identify different parts of a flowering plant: stamen, leaf, etc. He passes out a schematic diagram of a flower. The students are told to label the parts of the flower, seeking help from the book when they need it. Students who finish within twenty minutes are permitted to label another flower diagram. However, this time they may also paint the diagram with watercolors provided for this purpose. All the papers are turned in and after class, during the conference period, Mr. Nature selects the prettiest diagrams and places them on his bulletin board.

____ I- 2. *Effective Instructional Principles.* The following twelve instructional objectives provide an opportunity to differentiate between pairs of teachers according to which more effectively (presumptive effectiveness) employs a particular learning principle. Choose whether Teacher A or Teacher B more effectively uses the instructional principle in question.

Principle: Revelation of Objectives

1. a. Teacher A presents her second-grade class with a complete set of objectives for all subject areas at the beginning of the school year and urges them to consult this document frequently as the year progresses.

   b. Teacher B presents her second-grade students with only a few objectives every two or three weeks. In each case, she briefly explains what the objectives mean and gives sample test items for each one.

2. a. Teacher A provides his fifth-grade class with exactly the same set of explicitly stated instructional objectives that he uses when discussing his course goals with his colleagues. Although these are stated technically, the teacher believes that the students must

have access to the most accurate statements of the instructor's intentions if they are to comprehend the course objectives fully.

b. Teacher B uses a set of technically accurate instructional objectives but he modifies the language so that his fifth-grade students are more comfortable with that language. He is often forced to give several examples of test items in order to clarify the meaning of the objectives, but he believes the students understand his goals better as a result of this procedure.

3. a. Teacher A provides a set of behaviorally stated objectives for his ninth-grade biology students at the outset of the class and, every month thereafter, he reminds the students of the objectives they are pursuing during that month.

b. Teacher B believes that the students may be too distracted by specificity, and so each month he provides general goals such as the following for his students: "The class will become familiar with the process of photosynthesis."

Principle: Perceived Purpose

4. a. Teacher A initiates his unit on the American Revolution in a manner clearly designed to show the reasons for its occurrence. He spends considerable time outlining the social factors that precipitated the Revolution as well as the philosophical thought underlying the action of the American colonies. He is careful to point out how the English had actually allowed the colonies a high degree of autonomy and that freedom was a reality even before hostilities began.

b. Teacher B also initiates his study of American history with a discussion of the American Revolution, but his main emphasis is upon the points of tangency which the American Revolution shares with all other revolutions. He pays particular attention to relating this momentous event in our history to the problems of the emerging nations today.

5. a. Teacher A, in her eleventh-grade English class, introduces the students to the study of literary devices by explaining that they will be valuable for the reading which they will do in the future. She then carefully defines and gives examples of each term, instructing the students to copy the term and its meaning in their cumulative notebooks.

   b. Teacher B explains that literary terms are an important facet of the critic's vocabulary. She gives careful examples of each term from the class text after defining the word. In the discussion that follows, she carefully points out that the author makes his meaning much clearer to the reader by using the method that these terms merely describe.

6. a. Teacher A teaches her college-preparatory students algebra. In order to make them see how important the study of algebra really is, she exhorts her students to study since their successful completion of the course is prerequisite to their enrollment in a required plane geometry course which is normally a college requirement. She tries, by discussing its application, to show, more importantly, that algebra has intrinsic merit.

   b. Teacher B tells the students in his algebra class that they must learn to solve equations because the process will lead to competency in dealing with abstractions in the future and will enhance their power of logical thought.

Principle: Appropriate Practice

7. a. Teacher A, a music instructor, wants his choral group to sing five-part harmony in a satisfactory manner. He lets his class listen to records of great choral groups, pointing out what constitutes good and bad harmony.

After a number of these listening sessions, he allows the students time to discuss the components of good harmony. During the course of this discussion, Teacher A announces that the students will be required to start singing in class sometime next week.

b. Teacher B also wishes his choral group to sing harmoniously. However, his treatment of harmony, *per se*, is rather abridged. After playing only one selection of good harmony, he has his students sing simple songs and during this singing he points out those individuals who need to subdue the harsher qualities of their voices and those who need to increase the volume of their voices in order to insure proper blending of tone.

8. a. Teacher A, a physics teacher, wants his class to be able to solve some problems related to the velocity of a given projectile. In order to do so, they must have computational experience with given formulae. Teacher A presents the necessary information to the class and then allows them to apply these formulae to ten homework problems.

b. Teacher B also wants his students to solve velocity problems. However, he allows his students to experiment with different formulae without supplying cues as to which are correct. The students are given ten problems and told to use the formulae they believe to be correct. They are also told they will be given a five-problem quiz the next day.

9. a. Teacher A, Mr. Jacques, instructs a tenth-grade boys' physical education class. He wants his pupils to exhibit good sportsmanship in competitive athletics. He reads extensive sportsmanship essays to the class, most of which were written by sports idols such as Mark Spitz, Vida Blue, and Johnny Unitas. He then has the class choose teams and lets them play basketball on a

minor tournament scale for the remainder of the four-week unit. Team membership remains the same throughout the unit, with the most successful team being given a trophy at the conclusion of the tourney.

b. Teacher B, Mr. Swett, is an eleventh-grade P.E. instructor who also wants his boys to exhibit good sports-manship. He gives frequent lectures on the subject and makes sure to choose teams so that squads are evenly matched. During a three-week class tourney in basketball, he asks students to select the individuals who manifest the best sportsmanship in the class and to choose an All-Star team at the close of the tournament.

Principle: Knowledge of Results

10. a. Teacher A, in her English class, administers spelling tests every Thursday. In order to expedite the correction of these papers, she asks the students to exchange tests and grade them for each other according to her directions. The papers are immediately collected, grades are recorded, and a list is posted the following morning indicating the grades received by each student.

b. Teacher B allows her students to exchange papers for grading during their regular Thursday morning spelling tests. However, instead of collecting the papers immediately, she allows them to be passed back briefly to the owners and then collected. She returns the papers to the students the following morning after verifying and recording the grading done by their classmates.

11. a. Teacher A gives his social studies class an essay question on an examination. At the conclusion of the testing period, he collects the papers and then randomly selects students to present their answers to the test

question. Teacher A remarks that all these answers are interesting and creative.

b. Teacher B also administers an essay test question to her social studies class. The test is purposely timed so that after the papers have been collected, Teacher B can briefly enumerate those points which she felt essential that her students mention on their test paper.

12. a. Teacher A gives his students a multiple-option quiz. After collecting the papers, he immediately posts a correct answer sheet, listing: 1. A, 2. C, 3. A, 4. B, etc., in order that the students may know the correct answers.

b. Teacher B uses the multiple-choice quiz in the instruction of his students and, after collecting the papers, he immediately posts an examination booklet which makes both the question and the correct answer visible to his students.

_____ I- 3. *Teaching Assignments.* Students should be given several assignments to teach short lessons, such as ten-minute sessions, to fellow students or, if possible, to public school students comparable to those they will eventually teach. Insofar as the situation permits, the assignment should require the use of the main elements of the instructional paradigm. An observation form like the one provided in Part 9 of this text (page 105) can be useful in guiding the student's preparation.

_____ I- 4. *Instructional Techniques.* Select the teacher (a or b) who is *not* violating one of the instructional rules associated with the technique under consideration.

1. Lecturing

a. Teacher A, a junior high school biology instructor, employs a lecture approach in his classes of 100 to 150 students. Because of the size of the class, he tries to speak in such a way that the group will pay attention to his remarks. For instance, he speaks in a relatively loud, yet quite conversational fashion, maintaining frequent eye contact with members of the class. Because he believes large lecture classes tend to "fall asleep" unless the lecturer does something stimulating, he makes certain to introduce at least three humorous stories during each lecture from an anthology of after-dinner jokes.

b. Teacher B, an eleventh-grade English teacher, uses a lecture approach for several rather extensive sections of her homogeneously grouped, high-ability class. She always introduces questions in her lectures, some rhetorical and some for which she really wants answers. These questions tend to keep the students attentive to her presentation. Teacher B usually employs relatively short sentences and always explains new words. With her high-ability class, however, this is not often necessary. Each lecture is always summarized by Teacher B in the closing moments of the class.

2. Leading a Discussion

a. History Teacher A believes a discussion in his tenth-grade class is always more productive than a lecture. Accordingly, he prepares carefully for the frequent discussions that have become a trademark of this teacher's style. He outlines the questions he will ask and the probable conclusions he will summarize at the close of the discussion. Because he believes students respond best to topics when they are fresh and new, he announces each day's discussion topic at the beginning of the class period and capitalizes on the spontaneity of the student's responses.

b. History Teacher B attempts to use full-period discussions during his course when he believes the topic is sufficiently significant to justify the somewhat time-consuming nature of such sessions. This instructor found it necessary to devote several days at the beginning of the course to giving the students instruction in how to take part in a discussion. He invariably selects value-laden questions for discussion topics and, while he forces no final conclusion on all of the class, he tries to summarize the various views of the students at the end of each discussion.

3. Demonstrating

   a. Chemistry Teacher A demonstrates the use of the Bunsen burner during an early class session. He proceeds step by step, ascertaining frequently whether the class is comprehending the major points in the demonstration. He stresses safety precautions involved in the use of the gas required for the burner.

   b. Chemistry Teacher B demonstrates how to mix hydrochloric acid and various other chemical compounds. Before each demonstration he makes certain that all of the requisite equipment is available. Because of the dangers associated with the use of the acid, he does not allow students themselves to mix any of it.

4. Questioning

   a. Speech Teacher A poses frequent questions to his class regarding the quality of their own and others' speaking performance. He tries to emphasize the significance of each student's answer by briefly reiterating it in a slightly different way. He always addresses his questions to the whole class.

   b. Speech Teacher B tries to adapt his questions to the intellectual level of the students and, although he frequently poses the inquiry for the entire class, he usually tries to select a student for whom he thinks the question suitable. The teacher is particularly careful to treat student responses tactfully.

_____ I- 5. *Teaching Units.* List and, if you wish, briefly describe the recommended elements that should be included in a teaching unit.

1.

2.

3.

4.

5.

6.

7.

_____ I- 6. *Lesson Plans.* List and, if you wish, briefly describe the recommended elements that should be included in a lesson plan.

1.

2.

3.

4.

5.

_____ I- 7. *Instructional Plans.* In each of the following questions an operation will be described. Indicate by the letter of the correct answer whether the operation should be carried on in the preparation of (a) teaching units, (b) lesson plans, (c) both, or (d) neither.

1. Teacher and learner activities are detailed with time estimates provided in minutes.

2. A back-up lesson is recommended.

3. Criterion check is a required element.

4. A pre-test is included.

5. The instructional planner consults other sources to determine whether curricular restrictions are present.

6. Behavioral objectives are employed.

7. The teacher focuses on the question: "What should I do?"

8. Instructional resources are listed.

9. The teacher focuses on the question: "What do I want the learners to become?"

10. Broad, general objectives are often used here for organizational purposes.

_____ I- 8. *Discipline.* List at least four general principles and at least ten specific disciplinary techniques that might be of use to a teacher who is faced with an obstreperous child.

General Principles:
1.
2.
3.
4.

Specific Techniques:
1.
2.
3.
4.
5.
6.
7.
8.
9.
10.

_____ I- 9. *Instructional Terminology.* Select the term or phrase that best matches the definition.

1. A stimulus which, when removed from a situation, increases the probability of occurrence of the response it follows is known as
   a. a negative reinforcer
   b. a positive reinforcer
   c. punishment
   d. none of the above

2. An intermediate objective that must be mastered by a student on his way to achieving a more ultimate objective is called
   a. terminal behavior

b. en route behavior

c. entry behavior

d. preassessment

3. Providing practice for the learner during an instructional sequence so that he makes responses that are comparable but not identical to the responses called for in the instructional objective is referred to as

a. equivalent practice

b. entry behavior

c. analogous practice

d. positive reinforcement

EVALUATION

_____ E- 1. *Evaluative Decisions.* For the following exercises, decide which alternative is the most accurate interpretation of the situation.

1. Although students perform rather poorly on objective measures of their achievement, the anonymous questionnaires they filled out at the close of their course indicate that the instructor is "outstanding," "brilliant," and "the best teacher they've ever had." The instructor should infer from this information that

a. his instruction was acceptable and no major modifications should be made

b. deficiencies in pupil performance warrant modifications in his instructional plan

c. pupil evaluations far outweigh objective estimates of their performance

2. Although she failed to pre-test the students at the beginning of the semester, an elementary school teacher is rather satisfied with their mathematics performance at the close of the semester. Her satisfaction is

a. indefensible because of a failure to assess the learner's entry behavior

    b. thoroughly appropriate in view of their fine performance

    c. neither of the above

3. At the end of a unit of instruction, the teacher notes that his pupils' performance is well below what he expected. A reasonable interpretation of this result would be that

    a. there were inadequacies in instruction

    b. the objectives may not be appropriate for the learners

    c. his expectations regarding the performance associated with each objective have been unrealistic

    d. all of the above

_____ E- 2. *Testing Procedures.* Which of the following practices would be generally approved by evaluation and measurement specialists?

1. A teacher generally prefers multiple-choice items over true-false items when constructing objectively scorable tests.

2. This teacher contends that essay tests are generally unreliable because of both scorer reliability and sampling unreliability.

3. In judging the quality of a test item for purposes of measuring his objective, the instructor employs a content-validity rather than criterion-validity approach.

4. Typical item-analysis procedures are characteristically used by this teacher only with norm-referenced tests.

5. When faced with a shortage of time, this instructor uses item-sampling procedures in constructing his exams.

6. An elementary teacher uses the term "percentile" to represent the proportion of students who pass a test.

7. Mr. Hill believes that if a test is reliable, it must, of necessity, be valid.

8. This teacher believes that there is essentially no difference in the reliability associated with objectively and subjectively scored tests.

9. Most standardized tests represent exemplary instances of criterion-referenced measurement.

10. This teacher believes that "test-item distractors" are his colleagues who bother him when he is writing an examination.

_____ E- 3. *Criterion Measures.* Using the four-category scheme, classify each of the following items by writing in the appropriate letter. The classes of criterion measures are (a) learner behavior—natural conditions, (b) learner behavior—manipulated conditions, (c) learner product—natural conditions, and (d) learner product—manipulated conditions.

1. school attendance records

2. Stanford Achievement Test scores

3. written essay examinations dealing with "weakness and recommended changes in the elementary school's student government"

4. an examination of the annual tonnage of school litter found in the halls as an index of school citizenship

5. springboard diving in a district-wide meet

6. final extemporaneous speeches in senior English class

7. "courtesy" as reflected by adolescent boys giving their seats on the bus to women who might otherwise be obliged to stand

8. scores on a test of avocational interest

9. instances of pupil's "sportsmanlike conduct" during play periods

10. student essay examinations

_____ E- 4. *Writing Test Items.* Write at least two test items that are congruent with the following instructional objective: "The learner will be able to identify any punctuation errors in relatively simple sentences. These may be errors of omission or of commission with respect to the use of commas, semicolons, periods, and exclamation marks."

_____ E- 5. *Criterion- and Norm-Referenced Measurement.* Indicate, by writing in a *C* or *N*, whether the following operations, measurement devices, or measurement situations seem most appropriate for norm-referenced (*N*) or for criterion-referenced (*C*) measurement.

1. Reporting scores in terms of percentiles.

2. You want to construct a test that will identify the forty pupils in your school who have the most positive attitude toward minority-group teachers.

3. Test constituted by item sampling to measure achievement of course goals.

4. A nationally standardized group I.Q. test.

5. A pregnancy test.

6. You are a first-grade teacher who suddenly has available five well-trained tutors from the district high school. You want to construct a test that will identify the ten least able readers so that the tutors can work with them.

7. Designing test items so that they produce maximum score variability.

8. Reporting scores in terms of "percentage of items correct."

9. You want to write a test to help you determine how well you have been teaching your college history course.

10. A test of academic aptitude used for predicting college grade-point average.

____ E- 6. *Item Sampling.* Describe in a paragraph the basic procedure for making up tests by item sampling, and then describe the reasons why one would wish to use this approach.

____ E- 7. *Grading.* Identify, by checking the item, any of the following grading practices that are consistent with a criterion-referenced approach to instruction.

1. At the end of a particularly effective instructional year, Mr. Smith gives nothing but A's and B's in his class.

2. Mr. Swav has persuaded the school board to use a pass-fail system rather than the A,B,C,D,F scheme, and he finds in using such a scheme that only 5 percent of his students fail.

3. Mr. Hicks, to maintain high standards, always awards at least 10 percent D's and 10 percent F's in his class.

4. Miss Jolson is particularly attentive to the entry behavior of learners in items of their natural ability. She tries to adjust their grades so that if a student is achieving close to his maximum potential, he can receive relatively high grades in the class.

5. During a school year in which evidence indicates that he is rather ineffectual as an instructor, Mr. Hicks decides to give students the benefit of the doubt and awards them higher grades than might have been the case had he been teaching effectively.

____ E- 8. *Evaluation Terminology.* Select the term or phrase that best matches the definition.

1. The attempt to improve an instructional program before it is finally completed through an attempt to gather data and interpret this information with respect to the program's effectiveness is referred to as

    a. summative evaluation

    b. formative evaluation

    c. item analysis

    d. criterion validity

2. Measurement designed to assess an individual's standing with respect to other individuals on the same measuring device is referred to as

    a. norm-referenced measurement

    b. criterion-referenced measurement

    c. correlation

    d. content validity

3. The consistency with which a test measures whatever it is measuring is referred to as its

    a. reliability

    b. validity

    c. correlation

    d. percentile

Part 6

Appraising Instructional Objectives

One of the effective teacher's most important concerns is that his instructional expertise be directed toward the accomplishment of the right kinds of goals. One helpful technique for appraising the quality of instructional goals is to apply various classification scales devised for rating educational objectives to your goals in order to determine which behavior domain they fall in and to locate their level in that domain. The most widely used taxonomies are those developed by Bloom and his associates[1] and by Krathwohl and his associates.[2] The handbook on the cognitive domain was published in 1956. Although it received little attention for the first few years after it was published, it has been widely used since the 1960's. In 1964 a taxonomy dealing with the affective domain was published. Because of the general interest in instructional objectives during the 1960's, the affective taxonomy received instant attention and has enjoyed considerable use ever since. There is also a classification of educational objectives dealing with the psychomotor domain prepared by E.J. Simpson.[3]

---

[1]Bloom, Benjamin S. *et al.*, *Taxonomy of Educational Objectives, Handbook I: Cognitive Domain* (New York: David McKay, 1956).

[2]Krathwohl, David R. *et al.*, *Taxonomy of Educational Objectives, Handbook II: Affective Domain* (New York: David McKay, 1964).

[3]Simpson, E.J., *The Classification of Educational Objectives: Psychomotor Domain* (Urbana: University of Illinois, 1966).

A recent formulation by Robert M. Gagné, one of America's preeminent educational psychologists, is also helpful in classifying objectives.[4] Gagné describes six classes of objectives that can be used to reflect six different types of learning. In the remainder of this section we will consider these four classification schemes in more detail.

THE COGNITIVE DOMAIN

The cognitive domain deals with the ways in which an individual acquires and uses knowledge. In the book on the cognitive taxonomy, Bloom and his associates attempt to define and categorize the ways in which information is used and in doing so developed a scale that ranges from simple, concrete behavior through complex, more abstract behavior. At the lowest level of the taxonomy is knowledge.

KNOWLEDGE.   Knowledge basically consists of the recall of universals or specifics, of processes or methods, or of structures, patterns, and so forth. The essential attribute of this level of the taxonomy is *recall*. In other words, the knowledge level of the cognitive taxonomy describes learner activities that basically deal with memory or recollection. The knowledge level is further subdivided into

Knowledge of Specifics
Knowledge of Terminology
Knowledge of Specific Facts
Knowledge of Ways and Means of Dealing with Specifics
Knowledge of Conventions
Knowledge of Trends and Sequences
Knowledge of Classifications and Categories
Knowledge of Criteria
Knowledge of Methodology
Knowledge of the Universals and Abstractions in a Field
Knowledge of Principles and Generalizations
Knowledge of Theories and Structures

---

[4]Gagné, Robert M., *Defining Objectives for Six Types of Learning* (Washington, D.C.: American Educational Research Association, 1971). Adapted with the author's permission from a research training tape prepared for AERA.

COMPREHENSION. The second level of the taxonomy is comprehension, which represents the lowest non-rote form of understanding. At this level a learner knows what information is being communicated and is able to make use of it without necessarily seeing it in its fullest implications or relating it to other material. The comprehension level is subdivided into

Translation
Interpretation
Extrapolation

APPLICATION. At the application level of the cognitive taxonomy the learner uses abstractions in concrete or specific situations. Such abstractions might include general ideas, procedural rules, or generalized methods. The abstractions might also be technical principles or theories that must be recalled and applied. Bloom and his colleagues did not subdivide the application category, although they suggested that in writing measurement items to assess this cognitive level, the emphasis should be on devising situations that are new to the student. They suggested that this could be done by (1) presenting a fictional situation, (2) using material to which the student was not likely to have had previous exposure, or (3) taking a new slant on situations that might appear common to the group being tested.

ANALYSIS. Behavior on the analysis level involves breaking down a communication into its constituent parts in such a way that the relationship of ideas is made clear or, if a hierarchy of ideas is present, in a way that clarifies the hierarchy. Such analyses are intended to clarify communication by indicating how the communication is organized and the manner in which it conveys its effect. The analysis category is subdivided into

Analysis of Elements
Analysis of Relationships
Analysis of Organizational Principles

SYNTHESIS. Synthesis involves blending elements and parts in order to form a whole. This essentially involves working with parts, pieces, elements, and reorganizing them in such a way as to constitute a structural pattern that was not previously present. The synthesis category is subdivided into

Production of a Unique Communication
Production of a Plan or Proposed Site of Operations
Derivation of a Set of Abstract Relations

EVALUATION. At the highest level of the cognitive taxonomy we find evaluation. Evaluation involves judgments made about the value of methods and materials for particular purposes. Qualitative and quantitative judgments about the extent to which a certain phenomena satisfy given criteria are made. The criteria applied may be determined by the learner or given to him by someone else. The evaluation category is subdivided into

Judgments in Terms of Internal Evidence
Judgments in Terms of External Criteria

THE AFFECTIVE DOMAIN

The affective domain deals with values, attitudes and appreciations. The *Taxonomy of Educational Objectives, Cognitive Domain* by Krathwohl and his associates assumes that the pattern involved in acquiring values moves from a very low level of awareness toward the highest level of internalization. Even though the instructional procedures needed to promote goals in the affective domain are not fully understood, this hierarchy of affective behaviors is of considerable value to the educator. At the lowest level of the affective taxonomy we find receiving.

RECEIVING (ATTENDING). The initial level of the affective taxonomy is concerned with the learner's sensitivity to the existence of certain phenomena and stimuli and his willingness to receive or attend to them. Krathwohl and his associates identified this as the first crucial step if a learner is to acquire other skills intended by the teacher. This category is subdivided into

Awareness
Willingness To Receive
Controlled or Selected Attention

RESPONDING.   At the second level of the affective taxonomy we are concerned with responses that go beyond merely attending to phenomena. The student is sufficiently concerned with the stimuli. He is not simply willing to attend, but he is actively attending. Many teachers use this level of the affective taxonomy to describe "interest" objectives. We frequently use the term to describe the attitude of an individual who has become sufficiently involved with a subject or activity to seek it out. The responding level is subdivided into

> Acquiescence in Responding
> Willingness to Respond
> Satisfaction in Response

VALUING.   The third level of the affective taxonomy employs a descriptive term that is in common use by many educators. It is used in its ordinary sense, namely, to indicate that a thing, phenomenon, or behavior has worth to someone. This category describes many objectives that use such terms as "attitude" and "values." The valuing category is subdivided into

> Acceptance of a Value
> Preference for a Value
> Commitment

ORGANIZATION.   When learners internalize values, they encounter instances in which more than one value pertains. This situation requires the individual to organize such values into some kind of cohesive system. As the organized value system emerges, it becomes necessary to both conceptualize the values and establish their hierarchical relationship. Accordingly, the organizational category is subdivided into

> Conceptualization of a Value
> Organization of a Value System

CHARACTERIZATION.   At the highest level of the affective taxonomy we find the individual acting consistently in accordance with values he has previously accepted. The influence of these organized values is so pervasive that it is possible to characterize an individual in relationship to these values. For example, we might think of an individual who is so ardently liberal in his values that we can really describe him as a "liberal" in all realms of activity. The characterization level of the affective taxonomy is subdivided into

Generalized Set
Characterization

THE PSYCHOMOTOR DOMAIN

The psychomotor domain is concerned with the development and use of the muscles and the body's ability to coordinate its movements. *The Classification of Educational Objectives: Psychomotor Domain* by E.J. Simpson categorizes this area.

PERCEPTION. The first step in performing a motor act is the process of becoming aware of objects, qualities, or relations through the sense organs. It is the main portion of the situation-interpretation-action chain leading to motor activity.

SET. Set is a preparatory adjustment for a particular kind of action or experience. Three distinct aspects of set have been identified—mental, physical, and emotional.

GUIDED RESPONSE. This is an early step in the development of a motor skill. The emphasis is on the abilities that are components of the more complex skill. Guided response is the overt behavioral act of an individual under the guidance of another individual.

MECHANISM. At this level the learner has achieved a certain confidence and degree of skill in the performance of an act. The habitual act is a part of his repertoire of possible responses to stimuli and the demands of situations where the response is appropriate.

COMPLEX OVERT RESPONSE. At this level, the individual can perform a motor act that is considered complex because of the movement pattern required. The act can be carried out efficiently and smoothly, that is, with minimum expenditure of energy and time.

GAGNÉ'S CLASSIFICATION OF OBJECTIVES BY TYPES OF LEARNING

Robert Gagné has identified six types of objectives appropriate for describing intellectual skills we hope to produce in learners. Each of these types of objectives is associated with a different kind of learning. This scheme is helpful in appraising the quality of instructional objectives under consideration for an instructional sequence.

In Gagné's six-category system, the *major verb* is the key descriptor because it identifies the kind of intellectual operation being carried out by the learner. The learner can display the requisite skill by any number of overt behaviors, which are described by a variety of *minor verbs*. For example, an objective might be stated as follows:

> The learner will be able to *reinstate* [major verb] the names
> of the current Justices of the Supreme Court by *writing* [minor
> verb] them without prompts.

The minor verb in this objective could also have been *saying* the names, *listing* the names, or any other "ing" verb that would suggest an appropriate way for the student to demonstrate that he possessed the skill called for in the objective.

REINSTATING.   The learner reinstates a verbal or motor stimulus, such as reciting a poem he has memorized or performing the basic operations involved in tying a shoelace. This kind of learning is called *chain learning*. In such learning, the student becomes able to reel off a sequence of individual responses, either motor or verbal. For example, the motions required for buttoning a button or printing the letter K constitute motor chains. Memorized word sequences, such as "Two heads are better than one," are also verbal chains.

DISCRIMINATING.   The learner discriminates between two or more stimulus objects, usually objects that resemble each other to some extent. The type of learning involved is discrimination learning, which means that the learner is able to discern the difference between two or more objects —that is, he can tell whether two things are alike or different.

IDENTIFYING.   Gagné's third category of objectives requires the student to identify a concept, such as an object quality like *green* or *rectangular*, by its appearance. The type of learning involved here is *concrete concept learning*. In such learning, a child would be able to distinguish between the letters b and d after he had identified them in given words.

CLASSIFYING.   Gagné's fourth category of objectives requires the learner to classify, which should be understood to mean "classify by using a definition." Most of the concepts learned in school fall into this category, and the type of learning involved is called *defined concept* learning. Concepts, such as *society* or *culture*, have to be defined and cannot be denoted by simply pointing to them. This type of objective obliges the learner to use a definition rather than to simply recall (reinstate) information.

DEMONSTRATING.   The learner demonstrates that he knows a given rule. For instance, if the rule under consideration is "water flows downhill," then the learner must somehow show that he knows what the rule means. The kind of learning involved is called *rule learning*. Although there is not much difference between defined concepts and rules, definitions are one class of rules—that is, a rule that has the purpose of identifying a class of objects. An example of a suitable objective for this class of learning behavior might be, "Given a pair of dissimilar fractions, demonstrate the rule for their multiplication."

GENERATING.   The final class of objectives provided by Gagné uses the verb *generate*. It is associated with higher order rule learning. Such rules consist of two or more simpler rules. Such rules are not simply applied or demonstrated but are, in a sense, invented by the learner. The learner solves problems in novel situations. For instance, if we present to a child a brand-new problem of explaining why shadows cast at noon are shorter than those cast in the afternoon, then the learner has to put together several simple rules in order to discover a higher order rule.

REVIEW

For many educators, the most useful feature of the cognitive taxonomy is its emphasis on non-memory objectives. Too many teachers were pursuing goals which, even classified with generosity, fell into the lowest level of the cognitive taxonomy. For those teachers who recognized this, and cared, the cognitive taxonomy offered a scheme for emphasizing higher order intellectual behaviors. The publication of the affective taxonomy eight years later similarly reminded many educators that they were emphasizing cognition at the expense of affect.

Categorization systems such as those described in the foregoing pages can help educators become more circumspect in the selection of curricular emphasis. The more possible goals a teacher is aware of, the greater the likelihood that he will be able to create defensible goals.

Part 7

Glossary

Included in this glossary are brief descriptions of terms that are commonly used in connection with curricular, instructional, and evaluative considerations. Although the definitions of various terms are accurate, they are extremely terse. Thus, the interested reader may wish to pursue more technical definitions of these terms in advanced texts.

CURRICULUM

Affective: A term which describes behavior or objectives of an attitudinal, emotional, or interest nature, and which is discussed in the *Taxonomy of Educational Objectives: Handbook II, The Affective Domain* by David Krathwohl and others.

Behavioral Objectives: This term describes an instructional intent in such a way that the post-instructional behavior of the learner is described. What the learner should do, or be able to do, at the conclusion of an instructional sequence is described.

Cognitive: An adjective referring to learner activities or instructional objectives concerned with *intellectual* activities and discussed in *The Taxonomy of Educational Objectives: Handbook I, The Cognitive Domain* by Benjamin S. Bloom and others.

Course of Study: A guide prepared by a professional group of a particular school or school system as a prescriptive guide to teaching a subject or area of study for a given grade or other instruction group.

Criterion: This word usually refers to the measure used to judge the adequacy of an instructional program. Ordinarily, it would be a test, broadly conceived, of the program's objectives.

Curriculum: A structured series of intended learning outcomes.

Lesson Plan: A teaching outline of the important points of a lesson for a single class period arranged in the order in which they are to be presented; it may include objectives, points to be made, questions to ask, references to materials, assignments, and so forth.

Psychomotor: This refers to learner activities or instructional objectives relating to physical skills of the learner, such as typing or swimming.

Resource Unit: A collection of suggested learning and teaching activities, procedures, materials, and references organized around a unifying topic or learner problem; it is designed to be helpful to teachers in developing their own teaching units.

Scope: The extent or range of content or objectives (or both) covered by a course or curriculum.

Sequence: The order in which content or objectives are arranged in the curriculum.

Subject: A division or field of organized knowledge, such as English or mathematics.

Syllabus: A condensed outline or statement of the main points of a course of study.

Teaching Unit: The plan developed with respect to a particular classroom by an individual teacher to guide the instruction of a unit of work to be carried out by a particular class or group of learners for a period longer than a single class session.

INSTRUCTION

Analogous Practice: This term describes the responses made by the learner during the instructional sequence which are comparable, but not identical, to those called for in the instructional objective.

Appropriate Practice: This expression refers to opportunities provided the learner during the instructional sequence to respond in a fashion consistent with that described in the instructional objective. (See *Analogous Practice* and *Equivalent Practice*.)

Constructed Response: This refers to a learner's response, either to criterion test items or to material in the instructional product, wherein he is obliged to make a response which he, himself, must generate, as opposed to choosing between responses that have been generated for him. For instance, when a student is obliged to construct a short essay, this would be an instance of constructed response. Short "fill-in" answers to questions are also classified as constructed responses.

Contingency Management: This generally refers to classroom schemes that are based on the learner's receiving some kind of positive reinforcement for particular learning attainments. For example, in some cases the child can secure coupons for achieving certain instructional objectives, the coupons later being redeemable for rewards the child wishes to receive.

Discipline: This term can be used in a variety of ways, but for most teachers it refers to the procedures by which classroom control and order are maintained.

En Route Behavior: The behavior(s) that the learner acquires as he moves through an instructional program from his original entry behavior to the desired terminal behavior.

Entry Behavior: Sometimes referred to as prerequisite behavior, this describes the learner's behavioral repertoire as he commences the instructional program.

Equivalent Practice: This refers to responses made by the learner during the instructional program which are *identical* to those called for in the instructional objectives.

Knowledge of Results: This expression refers to a scheme by which a learner is provided with information regarding the adequacy of his responses. Sometimes called "feedback" or "corrective feedback," knowledge of results is provided whenever the learner can find out whether his responses are appropriate or inappropriate.

Negative Reinforcer: A stimulus which, when *removed* from a situation, increases the probability of the response that it follows. For example, a teacher might find that releasing a child from some aversive situation (staying after school) would increase the likelihood of a particular response of the child. (Negative reinforcement is not to be confused with punishment.)

Perceived Purpose: Promoting the child's realization of the worth of a particular subject he is studying or an objective he is attempting to accomplish.

Positive Reinforcer: A stimulus which, when *added* to a situation, increases the probability of the response it follows. For example, a teacher might find that verbal praise would increase the student's tendency to perform a particular classroom action.

Punishment: An aversive act that occurs after a particular response and is designed to diminish the frequency of the response it follows.

Selected Response: In selected responses, the learner chooses among alternatives presented to him, as when he selects multiple-choice responses, discriminates between true and false statements, and so on.

Task Analysis: The ordering of instructional objectives or en route behaviors to facilitate the attainment of instructional goals.

Terminal Behavior: The behavior that the learner is to demonstrate at the conclusion of the instructional program. What is terminal behavior in one program may, of course, be the initial behavior for a subsequent program.

EVALUATION

Content Validity: The degree to which a measuring device is *judged* to be appropriate for its purpose, for example, the degree to which it is congruent with a set of instructional objectives.

Correlation: The tendency for corresponding observations in two or more series to have similar relative positions.

Criterion-Referenced Measurement: Measurement designed to assess an individual's status with respect to a particular criterion or standard of performance, irrespective of the relationship of his performance to that of others.

Criterion Validity: Characteristically, the degree to which a particular measure, such as a test of intellectual ability, correlates with an external criterion such as subsequent scholastic performance in college.

Distractors: These are the alternatives or wrong answers in a multiple-choice or comparable test item.

Formative Evaluation: The evaluation of an instructional program before it is finally completed—that is, the attempt to evaluate a program in order to improve it.

Item Analysis: Any one of several methods used in revising a test to determine how well a given item discriminates among individuals or different degrees of ability or among individuals differing in some other characteristic.

Item Sampling: The procedure of administering different forms of a test (characteristically, shorter forms), to different individuals, thereby reducing the time required for testing.

Norm-Referenced Measurement: Measurement designed to assess an individual's standing with respect to other individuals on the same measuring device.

Percentile (centile): The point in distribution of scores below which a certain proportion of the scores fall. For example, a student scoring at the seventieth percentile on a test would have exceeded the scores of 70 percent of those taking the test.

Reliability: The accuracy with which a measuring device measures something; the degree to which a test measures consistently whatever it measures.

Standardized Test: A test for which content has been selected and checked empirically, for which norms have been established, for which uniform methods of administering and scoring have been developed, and which may be scored with a relatively high degree of objectivity.

Summative Evaluation: The final evaluation of a program in which the results of the program are characteristically compared with results of comparable programs in order for selection to be made among competing instructional programs.

Validity: The extent to which a test or other measuring instrument fulfills the purpose for which it is used.

Part 8

Answers to Practice Exercises

This section contains the correct answers to all of the practice exercises in Part 5. When checking the answers for a given exercise, you should conceal the answers below so that you will not see, inadvertently, the answers to exercises that you have not yet completed.

CURRICULUM

C- 1. *Measurable Objectives:* 2 and 7 should be marked.

C- 2. *Writing Objectives:* The answers must include descriptions of observable learner behavior or a product resulting from learner behavior. For example, an acceptable answer for the first item might be, "The student will be able to identify from a previously unseen series of statements regarding the causes of wars those five most pertinent to the cause of the Civil War."

C- 3. *Content Generality:* 1, 4, 8, and 9 should be marked.

C- 4. *Performance Standards:* 1. S; 2. N; 3. C; 4. N; 5. S; 6. N; 7. N; 8. S; 9. C; 10. N.

C- 5. *Objective Domains:* 1. c; 2. b; 3. d; 4. a; 5. b; 6. c; 7. a; 8. d; 9. b; 10. a.

C- 6. *Taxonomic Level:* 1. a; 2. c; 3. b; 4. a; 5. c.

C- 7. *Generating Objectives:* The answers must satisfy the criteria listed above under C-2, and in this case they must also be classifiable in the affective domain.

C- 8. *Ends and Means:* 3 and 4 should be checked.

C- 9. *Tyler Rationale:* 1. f; 2. a; 3. c; 4. b; 5. b; 6. e; 7. f; 8. g; 9. a; 10. d.

C-10. *Preassessment:* 1. c; 2. c.

C-11. *Curriculum Terminology:* 1. a; 2. c; 3. a.

INSTRUCTION

I- 1. *Instructional Principles, Part A:* 1. b and c; 2. a and b; 3. b and c; 4. b and c; *Part B:* 1. a and b; 2. c; 3. b and d; 4. b; 5. d; 6. none; 7. b; 8. c.

I- 2. *Effective Instructional Principles:* 1. b; 2. b; 3. a; 4. b; 5. b; 6. a; 7. b; 8. a; 9. b; 10. b; 11. b; 12. b.

I- 3. *Teaching Assignments:* Use of an observation form like the one found in Part 9 (page 106) will aid in judging the degree to which specific instructional principles have been employed.

I- 4. *Instructional Techniques:* 1. b; 2. b; 3. a; 4. b.

I- 5. *Teaching Units:* 1. precise instructional objectives; 2. pre-test; 3. day-by-day activities; 4. criterion check; 5. post-test; 6. resources; 7. back-up lesson.

I- 6. *Lesson Plans:* 1. precise instructional objectives; 2. learner activities; 3. teacher activities; 4. time estimates; 5. assignments (if any).

I- 7. *Instructional Plans:* 1. b; 2. a; 3. a; 4. a; 5. a; 6. c; 7. d; 8. a; 9. c; 10. a.

I- 8. *Discipline:* Refer to pages 36–40 for the names and descriptions of the general principles and specific techniques.

I- 9. *Instructional Terminology:* 1. a; 2. b; 3. c.

EVALUATION

E- 1. *Evaluative Decisions:* 1. b; 2. a; 3. d.

E- 2. *Testing Procedures:* 1, 2, 3, 4, 5.

E- 3. *Criterion Measures:* 1. a; 2. d; 3. d; 4. c; 5. b; 6. b; 7. a; 8. d; 9. a; 10. d.

E- 4. *Writing Test Items:* Two examples of correct answers to the exercise are the following:

> *Example 1. Circle any incorrect punctuation in this sentence:* The boy, found his dog near the riverside.
>
> *Example 2. Add any punctuation required in this sentence:* Tell me George, was that really your dog?

E- 5. *Criterion- and Norm-Referenced Measurement:* 1. N; 2. N; 3. C; 4. N; 5. C; 6. N; 7. N; 8. C; 9. C; 10. N.

E- 6. *Item Sampling:* Consult page 46 for a description of the basic procedure and rationale for making up tests by item sampling.

E- 7. *Grading:* 1, 2, 4, 5.

E- 8. *Evaluation Terminology:* 1. b; 2. a; 3. a.

Part 9

Useful Forms

A Suggested Form for a Lesson Plan

Teacher's Name_____

Class:_____Period:_____Date:_____

Objective(s):_____

_____

_____

_____

Assignment:_____

TIME	TEACHER ACTIVITIES	STUDENT ACTIVITIES

INSTRUCTIONAL PARADIGM OBSERVATION FORM

Your Name_____ Teacher's Name _____

School_____Class_____Date of Observation _____

Objectives	Yes	No	Uncertain
Was the instructional objective(s) stated in behavioral terms.	___	___	___
Did the instructional objective(s) specify a *student* minimal level?	___	___	___
Did the instructional objective(s) specify a *class* minimal level?	___	___	___

Comments:

Pre-Assessment	Yes	No	Uncertain
At the outset of instruction, was an attempt made to ascertain the learner's current status with respect to the objective(s)?	___	___	___

Comments:

Selection of Learning Activities:

Principle	Activities clearly show no use	Activities possibly show use	Activities clearly show use	If clearly used, principle was employed:
Revelation of Objectives	___	___	___	Ineffectively___ Fairly Effectively___ Very Effectively___
Perceived Purpose	___	___	___	Ineffectively___ Fairly Effectively___ Very Effectively___
Appropriate Practice	___	___	___	Ineffectively___ Fairly Effectively___ Very Effectively___
Knowledge of Results	___	___	___	Ineffectively___ Fairly Effectively___ Very Effectively___

Comments:

Evaluation	Yes	No	Uncertain
At the conclusion of the learning activity, was the learner evaluated?	___	___	___
Was the evaluation appropriate for the specified objective(s)?	___	___	___

Comments:

Part 10

Selected Bibliography

CURRICULUM

BAKER, E.L., and W.J. POPHAM, *Expanding Dimensions of Instructional Objectives* (Englewood Cliffs, N.J.: Prentice-Hall, 1973).

BLOOM, B.S. *et al.*, *Taxonomy of Educational Objectives, Handbook I: Cognitive Domain* (New York: David McKay, 1956).

CLARK, D.C., *Using Instructional Objectives in Teaching* (Glenview, Ill.: Scott, Foresman, 1972).

EISNER, E.W., "Educational Objectives: Help or Hindrance?" *School Review* 75 (1967), pp. 250–66.

FRENCH, W., *et al.*, *Behavioral Goals of General Education in High Schools* (New York: Russell Sage Foundation, 1957).

GAGNÉ, R.W., "The Analysis of Instructional Objectives for the Design of Instruction." In R.L. Glaser, ed., *Teaching Machines and Programmed Learning, II, Data and Decisions* (Washington, D.C.: Department of Audio Visual Instruction, National Education Association, 1965), pp. 21–65.

HERRICK, V.E., and R.W. TYLER, eds., *Toward Improved Curriculum Theory.* Supplementary Educational Monographs, No. 71 (Chicago: University of Chicago Press, 1950).

KRATHWOHL, D.R., "Stating Objectives Appropriately for Program, for Curriculum and for Instructional Materials Development." *Journal of Teacher Education* 12 (1965), pp. 83–92.

_____, "The Taxonomy of Educational Objectives—Its Use in Curriculum Building." In C.M. Lindvall, ed., *Defining Educational Objectives* (Pittsburgh: University of Pittsburgh Press, 1964).

KRATHWOHL, D.R., *et al.*, *Taxonomy of Educational Objectives, Handbook II: Affective Domain* (New York: David McKay, 1964).

MAGER, R. F., *Goal Analysis* (Belmont, Calif.: Fearon Publishers, 1972).

_____, *Preparing Instructional Objectives* (Belmont, Calif.: Fearon Publishers, 1962).

POPHAM, W.J., ed., *Instructional Objectives* (Chicago: Rand McNally, 1969).

POPHAM, W.J., and E.L. BAKER, *Establishing Instructional Goals* (Englewood Cliffs, N.J.: Prentice-Hall, 1970).

INSTRUCTION

ARNSTINE, D.G., "The Language and Values of Programmed Instruction: Part 2." *The Educational Forum* 28 (1964), pp. 337–46.

ATKIN, J.M., "Some Evaluation Problems in a Course Content Improvement Project." *Journal of Research in Science Teaching* 1 (1963), pp. 129–32.

GAGNÉ, R.W., *The Conditions of Learning*, 2nd ed. (New York: Holt, Rinehardt & Winston, 1970).

_____, "Curriculum Research and the Promotion of Learning." In *AERA Monograph Series on Curriculum Evaluation*, Vol. I (Chicago: Rand McNally, 1967).

GLASER, R.L., "Ten Untenable Assumptions of College Instruction." *Educational Record* 49 (Spring 1968), pp. 154–59.

GLASER, R.L., ed., *Teaching Machines and Programmed Learning, II, Data and Decisions* (Washington, D.C.: Department of Audio Visual Instruction, National Education Association, 1965).

HYMAN, R.T., *Ways of Teaching* (Philadelphia: J.B. Lippincott, 1970).

JACKSON, P.E., *The Way Teaching Is* (Washington, D.C.: Association for Supervision and Curriculum Development, National Education Association, 1966).

JOYCE, B.R., MARSHA WEIL, and RHOADA WALD, *Basic Teaching Skills,* (Chicago: Science Research Associates, 1969).

KOMISAR, P.B., and J.E. MCCLELLAN, "Professor Arnstine and Programmed Instruction." *The Educational Forum* 29 (1965), pp. 467–76.

LUCIO, W.H., and J.D. MCNEIL, *Supervision: A Synthesis of Thought and Action* (New York: McGraw-Hill, 1969).

MAGER, R.F., *Developing Attitude Toward Learning* (Belmont, Calif.: Fearon Publishers, 1968).

PETER, L.J., *Prescriptive Teaching System Individual Instruction,* (New York: McGraw-Hill, 1972).

POPHAM, W.J., and E.L. BAKER, *Classroom Instructional Tactics* (Englewood Cliffs, N.J.: Prentice-Hall, 1973).

_____, *Designing an Instructional Sequence* (Englewood Cliffs, N.J.: Prentice-Hall, 1970).

_____, *Systematic Instruction* (Englewood Cliffs, N.J.: Prentice-Hall, 1970).

TYLER, R.W., *Basic Principles of Curriculum and Instruction* (Chicago: University of Chicago Press, 1950).

WALLEN, N.E., and R.M.W. TRAVERS, "Analysis and Investigation of Teaching Methods." In N.G. Gage, ed., *Handbook of Research on Teaching* (Chicago: Rand McNally, 1963).

EVALUATION

BLOOM, B.S., J.T. HASTINGS, and G.F. MADAUS, *Handbook on Formative and Summative Evaluation of Student Learning* (New York: McGraw-Hill, 1971).

CRONBACH, L.F., "Course Improvement Through Evaluation." *Teachers College Record* 64 (1963), pp. 672–83.

GLASER, R.L., "Instructional Technology and the Measurement of Learning Outcomes: Some Questions." *American Psychologist* 18 (1963), pp. 519–21.

HASTINGS, J.T., "Curriculum Evaluation: The Why of the Outcomes." *Journal of Educational Measurement* 3 (1966), pp. 27–32.

MCNEIL, J.D., "Antidote to a School Scandal." *The Educational Forum* 30 (1966), pp. 60–77.

POPHAM, W.J., *An Evaluation Guidebook* (Los Angeles: The Instructional Objectives Exchange, 1972).

POPHAM, W.J., and T.R. HUSEK, "Implications of Criterion-Referenced Measurement." *Journal of Educational Measurement* 6 (Spring 1969), pp. 1–9.

SANDERS, N.M., *Classroom Questions: What Kinds?* (New York: Harper and Row, 1966).

SCRIVEN, M., "The Methodology of Evaluation." In B.O. Smith, ed., *Perspectives of Curriculum Evaluation* (Chicago: Rand McNally, 1967).

STAKE, R.E., "The Countenance of Educational Evaluation." *Teachers College Record* 68 (1967), pp. 523–40.

STUFFLEBEAM, D.I., *et al., Educational Evaluation Decision Making* (Itasca, Ill.: F.E. Peacock, 1968).

WEBB, E.J., *et al., Unobtrusive Measures* (Chicago: Rand McNally, 1966).